Food for Pilgrims:
A Journey With Saint Luke

Revised Edition

Food for Pilgrims: A Journey With Saint Luke

Revised Edition

Dwight W. Vogel, O.S.L.

OSL Publications
Akron, Ohio

Food for Pilgrims:
A Journey with Saint Luke
Revised Edition

ISBN 1-878009-28-1

Produced and manufactured in the United States of America by
OSL Publications
P.O. Box 22279
Akron, Ohio 44302-0079

The Order of Saint Luke is a religious order dedicated to sacramental and liturgical scholarship, education and practice. The mission of the publishing ministry is to put into the hands of students and practitioners resources which have theological, historical, ecumenical and practical integrity.

CONTENTS

"Veni Sancte Spiritus"

Come, Holy Spirit, come;
Radiate your light divine.
Source of all gifts, come;
Shine within our hearts.

Great Comforter,
The soul's most welcome guest:
In labor you are rest,
In heat, coolness,
In woe, reassurance and relief.

O blessed Light,
Shine within our hearts and fill our inmost being.
Without you, nothing is free from taint of ill,
Nothing is good in thought or deed.

Heal what is wounded,
Strengthen what is weak,
Cleanse what is filthy,
Water what is parched,
Bend what is stubborn,
Melt what is frozen,
Warm what is chill,
Guide what is devious.

On the faithful who trust in you,
Pour out your sevenfold gifts;
Give us boundless mercy--
Your salvation--
Joy unending.
Amen.

Adapted by DWV from the thirteenth century prayer of Archbishop Stephen Langton
as translated by E. Caswall (1814-1878); Adapted from *The Daily Office: A Book of
Hours for Daily Prayer After the Use of the Order of Saint Luke*, © 1994 by the Order of
Saint Luke. Used by permission.

INTRODUCTION:

CONFESSIONS OF A PILGRIM

You are being invited to share a journey with me: a pilgrimage in which we discover what can feed us as we reflect on who we are called to be and what we are called to do. If we're going to share that journey, you might want to know something about the tour guide: who I am, what journey I'm on, and why I've chosen my experience with the Order of Saint Luke as a way of opening up the broader questions of liturgical spirituality which are of interest and concern for many beyond the Order. On this journey I've become aware of how important worship is to Christian discipleship, so I will be talking about what "liturgical spirituality" is, and why it is so important.

My father was an Evangelical United Brethren minister who served in the Kansas Conference. He loved the Bible, especially the psalms. I would often join my mother and father around the piano as we sang the hymns of the Church. Scripture and music were as important to my nurture as food and drink!

As a district superintendent for many years, Dad would take us along as he "traveled the district." There were still three week-long camp meetings in the district, as well as revival services, and a conference-wide "summer assembly." In my youth I played piano for many of those services. But something else was going on, too. Every camp meeting, every summer assembly included a celebration of holy communion. It was at a communion service that I first became aware of my call to "the ministry of the gospel." Those celebrations — in local church, camp meeting, and assembly — were stations of spiritual nurture along my pilgrim journey. These were not "high Church" liturgy in any way. They were evangelical in nature; that is, they proclaimed the good news of Jesus Christ and called for the response of faith. But they were also deeply sacramental. In them I found food for the journey.

I attended Westmar College in LeMars, Iowa, and there my horizons were broadened. On several occasions, there were joint services with the Methodist church downtown. The pastor wore a clerical collar, a robe, and a stole. When I asked about these things (so foreign to my experi-

1

ence), he explained their significance, and added that he was a member of the Order of Saint Luke. I was intrigued, but that was all.

After college, I did graduate work as a Danforth Fellow, first studying for an MA in philosophy of religion at Boston University, then taking my seminary degree at Andover Newton Theological School, and completing a doctorate in theology in the Northwestern University/Garrett Theological Seminary program. My wife and I sought significant worship experiences, and were surprised to find ourselves drawn to Trinity Episcopal Church in Copley Square while in Boston.

For twenty years, Linda and I were on the faculty at Westmar College. Early on, I was asked to take responsibility for the weekly Vespers service which was to be the "liturgical service" for the school. I started reading about worship, and discovered that liturgy was an area which really excited me. Among the periodicals, I often looked at *The Versicle* from the Order of Saint Luke.

Later I was appointed pastor of historic Saint Luke's United Methodist Church in Dubuque, Iowa. My years as pastor there were wonderfully fulfilling. I discovered that my ministry was centered in the worship of the Church, especially in the celebration of the sacraments. Noticing an invitation to inquire about the Order of Saint Luke, I sent off for information.

I discovered that the Order of Saint Luke was "a religious order in the United Methodist Church dedicated to sacramental and liturgical scholarship, education and practice." I could affirm the vows with heart-felt integrity.[1] They seemed to express a perspective I had been looking for. I professed those vows through the mail (there being no local chapter around), and shortly thereafter attended a national convocation of the Order. The Order put me in contact with others who were engaged in a similar pilgrimage of faith, persons who were being fed by the worship and sacraments of the Church.

Gradually I have recognized that my vocation is that of liturgical theologian. While pastor at Saint Luke's, I joined Bishop Rueben P. Job in leading workshops on the intersection of worship and spirituality. Preparation for those sessions, and interaction with Bishop Job as we led them, provided the core material out of which this book grew.

As a member of the faculty at Garrett-Evangelical Theological Seminary, I taught in areas which reflect that vocational identity: theology, worship, music ministry. The context for my teaching, peaching, and living involves a deeper dynamic. In retirement, as in my years of teaching and pastoring, I am nourished by a sacramental spirituality grounded in the liturgical life of the Church.

My participation in the Order of Saint Luke has helped me clarify the sources of this kind of nurture for my pilgrimage of faith, as well as for my life as a scholar. In 1991, I was invited to lead a series of sessions on liturgical theology for the national retreat of the Order. Preparing for those presentations brought me face to face with the need to clarify some unresolved questions in my own work. My education and interest in theology, liturgics, and spiritual formation convinced me that all three are (or at least ought to be) closely interrelated. I wanted to uncover that interrelationship.

Kevin Irwin gave me the clue in his observation that

what makes liturgy a unique source for theology is that it is a *ritual event* and therefore clearly distinguished from other theological sources, such as statements of the *magisterium* [that is, the official teachings of the Church]. Hence ... it is essential that we employ a hermeneutic [an interpretive process] that respects the event character of liturgy, especially liturgical language and liturgical action.[2]

Liturgy is more than a source for theology (though without a doubt it is that as well), but I found myself asking: "where in the life of the Order of Saint Luke can we find a ritual event which provides clues for a liturgical theology and spirituality which might inform us, guide us, and challenge us?" To put it another way: what can help us know who we are, what we are about, and within what context we live?

As I reflected on that question, I realized that the liturgical event which provides the answers to those questions most powerfully for me is the service of the profession and renewal of vows. There members of The Order are given not only a common language, but an *event* which can be a common point of departure.

Out of discussions within the Order about whether we ought to reflect one of the historic religious spiritualities (for example, Benedictine, Franciscan, Ignatian), I found myself looking instead for a spirituality inherent in the Order of Saint Luke. My journey toward the discovery of that kind of spirituality was greatly enriched by the conversations some of us shared at a retreat in Pittsburgh in 1994 where Barbara Troxell and Dan Benedict led members of the Order in considering further a spirituality which might grow out of the writings of Luke in the Gospel which bears his name and the Acts of the Apostles. During one of the times of silence, I reflected on those verses at the conclusion of Acts 2 which describe the life of the Church in the days following Pentecost and their resonance with the Rule of Life and Service of the Order of Saint Luke. Once again

I realized that the profession and renewal of vows is a ritual event for members of the Order which has come to have deep meaning for me as I seek to live a sacramental life. I became aware that I could find in these verses scriptural clues to the nature of a Lukan spirituality, *a spirituality that is not restricted to members of the Order.*

What I have tried to do in these pages is to help us think together about the nature of liturgical spirituality and the sacramental life when viewed through "Lukan lenses." I am not a New Testament scholar, however, but a liturgical theologian. This is not a scriptural study based on Luke-Acts, a fact that may disappoint some of you. Rather, it explores what happens when I let Luke/Acts resonate with the vows I have taken as a member of the Order of Saint Luke. "Lukan" as I am using it, parallels "Benedictine" or "Franciscan." It refers primarily to a "Lukan community" seeking greater clarity about our identity.

The writings of Saint Luke provide us with some important clues, and we will examine those in the first chapter. Out of that, some key themes emerge which help us develop a liturgical spirituality growing out of liturgical events in the life of the Church: baptism, eucharist, the daily office, and the pastoral offices. Finally, we will look back over our exploration together and note dynamics which enable the development of a theology of liturgical spirituality.

I am grateful to Bishop Rueben Job and to many of my brothers and sisters in the Order for the benefit of their insights. Walking the road with you has been a source of grace. It is my hope that this book will provide a basis for study and discussion not only among us, but for the wider Church as well.

There is another covenant relationship even more basic to the presence of God's grace in my life: my life partner, Linda, who is soul-friend, mentor, colleague, critic and lover. For her and for all who walk this journey of faith with me, I give thanks to God.

Dwight W. Vogel, OSL
Garrett-Evangelical Theological Seminary
The Feast of Saint Luke, 1995
Revised, The Feast of Saint Mary of Magdala, 2004

Endnotes
1. See Appendix A
2. Kevin W. Irwin, *Liturgical Theology: A Primer* (Collegeville, MN: The Liturgical Press, 1990), p. 18

One
Seeking a Lukan Spirituality

Like persons lost in a wilderness who nearly starve to death while there is nourishment all around them, we remain only partially aware of what can feed our souls. We have not learned where to look, and what to look for. The complex process of consciously naming something as "food" changes the way we interact with it. We need food for our spiritual journey, and I believe we can find that food in the worship life of the Church. Through a *liturgical spirituality*, we can be opened up to *sacramental living*, a way of living that taps the nourishment which, by God's grace, is all around us.

While the whole book is an exploration of the meaning of *liturgical spirituality* and *sacramental living*, let me provide some working definitions to get us on our way. The word "spirituality" is one of those words which defies attempts at precise definition.[1] For me, *spirituality* refers to what nourishes our being, our thinking, and our doing, enabling our discipleship. It involves the "interior" and personal aspects of discipleship, but includes the "relational" or communal aspects, and reaches beyond the Christian community with "missional" implications as well. Spirituality has to do with our whole being. *Liturgical spirituality*, then, has to do with the way in which liturgy can provide nurture for our pilgrimage of faith.

What does it mean to *live sacramentally*? When we say something is sacramental, we are saying that it is an unusually transparent experience which reveals a Transcendent reality beneath and beyond and behind it. It is symbolic in the profound sense of that word. So living sacramentally is "being in touch" with sources for spirituality grounded in God's grace which lie "beyond" or "beneath" or "within" what appears to our senses, for example, the liturgy of the Church.

I yearn for foundations on which to build a spirituality which feeds my spiritual hunger. At the same time, I am keenly aware that I need to be in communion with other pilgrims with whom I share the journey. There are many approaches available; patterns of spirituality abound. We can learn much from Benedictine, Franciscan, Augustinian and Ignatian spirituali-

5

ties, to name a few.[2] However, none of those provide me with a "home base." They emerged out of contexts and were expressed through communities which are different from mine.

The ruminations which gave rise to this book began to develop in response to the question: "Why is the order to which you belong named after Saint Luke?" I appropriate this question, not at the level of historical inquiry, but rather at the level of theological reflection. *What is there in Luke-Acts which resonates with and informs my yearning for a liturgical spirituality — a spirituality which unites me with others seeking to live a sacramental life?* As I reflect on this question, I become aware that we can find in these New Testament writings scriptural clues that help us develop a Lukan spirituality.

We recall the tremendous impact which Saint Luke has exerted on the Daily Prayer of the Church through the evangelical canticles. These songs from the early chapters of Luke's gospel became closely associated with times of prayer in the Church's life: the Song of Zechariah (also known as the *Benedictus*, from Luke 1:68-79, sung at Morning Prayer), the Song of Mary (also known as the *Magnificat*, from Luke 1:46-55, sung at Evening Prayer), and the Song of Simeon (also known as the *Nunc Dimitis*, from Luke 2:29-32, sung at Night Prayer). These, together with the *"Gloria in excelsis"* (which starts with words from Luke 2:14) are rich resources for us. As we pray them, what do they tell us about the spirituality we share?

During a time of silence at a retreat, I became aware of the particular implications in Acts 2:42-47 for liturgical spirituality and the sacramental life. Here are markers to guide our journey:

1. They devoted themselves to the teaching of the apostles.
(Acts 2:42a)

Concern for the "apostolic hope" must be based on the New Testament writings. The center of their teaching and preaching the "good news" (and the source of their hope and ours) is Jesus Christ. But this is not merely a general interest in Jesus. It is focused on what the Church has called the "paschal mystery." Understanding of this mystery has broadened from a medieval emphasis on the crucifixion, to the death and resurrection, to the incarnation, life, death, and resurrection of Jesus *and* how Christian disciples participate in those realities. Joyce Anne Zimmerman has included Pentecost in that expanding vision.[3] Thus, we are concerned not merely with the teachings of the past, nor escaping into

6

a hope for the future, but with *the way we live into the future through remembering a past which transforms the present*.

Stories of the passion and resurrection comprise a great deal of Luke's gospel story. We might begin by looking at 9:18-50 (which puts the transfiguration story into the context of Jesus' approaching death), and then turn to 19:28 (which begins the story often called the "triumphal entry") and read through the end of the Gospel, to get some sense of the story. However, it is in Acts that we discover the way in which the "apostolic hope" is centered in the "paschal mystery." There is an "evangelical" nature inherent in an understanding of sacramental spirituality which takes the paschal mystery and the apostolic hope seriously.

The world is topsy-turvy and hostile. Yet we gather in hope, accepting and living by the promise of the abiding presence of God. This dimension of faith is in short supply and can be a gift to the whole Church. Apostolic hope is at the heart of Lukan spirituality.

2. They devoted themselves to . . . the *koinonia*.   (Acts 2:42b)

Community is an ongoing concern for our spirituality. What do we discover about *koinonia* in Luke and Acts? Can the stories in Acts help us discern what it means to be a community in dispersion? What understanding of the Church is inherent in those stories?

Lukan spirituality is not individualistic but essentially communal. We are called to "live for the Church of Jesus Christ." But where in the world of our experience *is* the Church? On the one hand, we get into trouble by focusing only on one particular congregation (which like the church at Corinth, is likely to be beset by sins and sinners of amazing diversity!). On the other hand, we can try to spiritualize the Church into a Platonic ideal unbesmirched by the world but, by that very fact, unable to be incarnated in our earthy and earthly communities. The Church is *both* the Church catholic at all times and in all places — the communion of the saints — *and* the people gathered at this time, in this place, with all their sins and foibles. We can ignore the blemishes of the saints of the past only if we don't look closely! As Luther knew, the Church is made up of people who are *simul justus et peccator* (both justified and a sinner).

I have chosen to transliterate the Greek word *koinonia* because it avoids the picture of superficial comraderie which "fellowship" engenders for some. It is a richer word, pointing to what we share — hopes, fears, sorrows, joys, tensions, harmony and dissonance, mutual nurture and support as well as pluralistic appropriations which threaten but also enrich our unity. Our common fidelity to the oneness of Christ in the Church is the basis of our unity.

Koinonia is also found when groups of Christians meet ("from house to house," as Luke puts it). Not all groups will share the same *"apostolate"* — the same sense of what they are sent out to do. Fundamental to the *koinonias* within *the Koinonia* we call the Church, is the need to discover the *"charisms"* or gifts which have been given to our particular band of disciples, and to discern the apostolate to which we are called.

3. They devoted themselves . . . to the breaking of bread.

(Acts 2:42c)

The sacraments are important for a Lukan spirituality. Luke provides us not only with stories of Jesus' baptism (3:21-22) and the "last supper" (22:1-38), but also with the appearance at Emmaus (24:13-35). It is a story of "real presence" which can transform our lives. For some of us, the apostolate we discern is that of being missioners of sacramental grace. Many of us function in ministry with colleagues for whom the sacraments, while a part of the church's life, are not at the heart of its life and mission. The call to "magnify the sacraments" is a call to recognize that if we can discern and appropriate the significance of our gathering as baptized disciples to celebrate Eucharist in Christ's name by the power of the Holy Spirit, we will uncover the underlying dynamic of evangelism, mission, outreach and service, as well as experiencing as sign and act what it means to be the body of Christ.

4. They devoted themselves to . . the prayers.   (Acts 2:42d)

It is the presence of the definite article "the" in the Greek which reminds us that Luke is not talking here about prayer in general. These are *"the* prayers" of the community, that is for us "the corporate worship of the Church." Alexander Schmemann has taught us that the mark of our humanity is our capacity for worship. We are *homo adorans*.[4] But much of the Church today is not too "devoted" to worship. There are other agenda which seem more urgent. There is pressure to replace worship with something else to meet the predilections of the target audience.

We are like the disciples facing the crowd. Jesus says: "give them something to eat" and we t think we have nothing to offer. But when the loaves and fish we find insufficient are *blessed* by Christ, they can nourish

8

us and all those in need. The revitalization of the Church awaits the discernment of a people committed to worshipping "in spirit and in truth" — with both vitality and integrity. The call is not to do what is "liturgically correct" because of its historic validity; it is to discover the vibrant depths of a liturgy which has sustained the Church through the ages and appropriate it for a people called to move into a future in which God's kin-dom will come and God's will be done. By speaking of *kin-dom*, I mean that reign of God in which all are kinfolk, brothers and sisters of one another.[5]

Our apostolic work is to live out (and encourage the Church to appropriate) a monastic insight: worship is the central act of the Church and is basic to sacramental living.

5. . . . and breaking bread from house to house, they shared food with glad and generous hearts.

(Acts 2:46b)

Baptism and the "breaking of bread" by the community are important parts of the story of the early Church told in Acts, but they have their roots in the stories told in Luke's gospel: Jesus' baptism (3:21-22), the "last supper" (22:1-38), and the appearance at Emmaus (24:13-35). What happens when we take the Emmaus road story, for example, and seek to find in it points of connection with our own story? How can that clarify the nature of a "sacramental spirituality?"

We are called to "live the sacramental life." We are to be "sacraments of the sacraments." And since baptism and Eucharist are sign-acts of God's grace in and through Jesus Christ, they are sacraments of THE Sacrament, Jesus Christ.[6] It is cumbersome to speak of being sacraments (embodiments) of the sacraments (Baptism and Eucharist) of *the* Sacrament (Christ), but that is the reality. For it is not enough to be baptized, or to receive the bread and cup. It is in living our baptism, in sharing "with glad and generous hearts" from day to day, from house to house, that we are the body of Christ.

6. . . . and distributed to all according to their need.

(Acts 2:45b)

Here the mysteries of grace meet God's preference for those who live on the margins of life. There is special concern in Luke's writings about groups who were often marginalized in his day: women (for example, Mary, Elizabeth, Anna, those who traveled with him, and those who witnessed his execution and resurrection), children (not only with regard to Jesus himself, but also in miracles of healing), and the poor and oppressed

9

see the following parables which belong exclusively to Luke: 7:41-43 (the two debtors), 11:5-8 (about giving), 12:13-21 (the unwise farmer); 15:8-10 (the lost coin); 16:19-31 (the rich man and Lazarus); 18:1-8 (the persistent widow). How do these concerns impact the way in which we live out our spirituality?

To "accept the call to service" operates in ever expanding circles. I must come to terms with what it means to be in service with and for those with whom I have made special covenants (for example, my marriage partner, my sisters and brothers in the Order). Then there is my service with and for others in my local congregation, in my community, in the Church universal, and in the world. The particular discernment of Luke, however, is that all this service should be distributed "according to their need." And it is precisely with the poor, the disenfranchised, and the marginalized that Luke is concerned.

Discerning our apostolate within our primary covenants *and* discerning our apostolate within the Church are important and ongoing tasks. However, it is ministry to the marginalized which a group of people committed to the vitality of worship and the importance of the sacraments may find most challenging, and yet living the sacramental life dare not exclude that kind of ministry.

The tradition speaks of Saint Luke as "the physician" and that concern for healing is part of his spirituality. Thus, in the collect for the Order of Saint Luke we pray "that we may bring your healing grace to the whole Church." We know that we have received healing as individuals and as a community. We know that we need healing still. Likewise the Church is a community of those who have been made whole, who are being made whole, and who will be made whole. As such we become channels of God's healing grace for the world.

First and last, then, this is the work of the Holy Spirit — a very Lukan conclusion. Therein lies the reason for the hymn which appears at the beginning and end of this book: *Veni, Sancte Spiritus!* (Come, Holy Spirit!)

There are more references to the Spirit in Luke than in Matthew and Mark combined! The stress is there from the beginning in reference to John the Baptist (1;15), Mary (1:35), Elizabeth (1:41), Zachariah (1:67), and Simeon (2:25-26). Jesus is conceived by the Spirit (1:35), baptized by the Spirit (3:22), and led into the wilderness to be tested by the Spirit (4:1). His ministry is empowered by the Spirit (4:14,18); he rejoiced in the Spirit (10:21) and promised his disciples they would be "clothed with power from on high" (24:49). The Book of Acts continues this theme by showing the work of the Holy Spirit in the life of the early Church. How can this emphasis on the work of the Spirit help us understand the nature of the spirituality we seek? The presence of the word *Spirit* within the word *spirituality* may serve to remind us of a deep truth.

Thanks be to God for the grace given us day to day to grow in a spirituality toward which the writings of Luke point the way! We turn to a further exploration of the nature of that pilgrimage and to a deeper understanding of these dimensions. *Veni, Sancte Spiritus!* (Come, Holy Spirit!)[7]

Endnotes

1. See the pages regarding spirituality in *The Study of Spirituality*, edited by Cheslyn Jones et al (New York: Oxford Press) 1986. One definition cited there states: "spirituality means a search for meaning and significance by contemplation and reflection on the totality of human experiences in relation to the whole world which is experienced and also to the life which is lived and may mature as that search proceeds." (Eric Jones, ed. *Spirituality for Today* (SCM, 1968), p. 61.

2. A helpful summary of these spiritualities appears in *Prayer and Temperament* by Chester P. Michael and Marie V. Norrisey (Charlottsville, VA: The Open Door) 1984.

3. Joyce Ann Zimmerman, *Liturgy as Living Faith: A Liturgical Spirituality* (London and Toronto: Associated University Presses) 1993.

4. Alexander Schmemann, *For the Life of the World,* Second revised edition. (Crestwood, NY: St. Vladimir's Seminary Press, 1973)

5. See Letty Russell, *Household of Freedom* (Philadelphia: Westminster Press) 1987.

6. See Edward Schillebeeckx, *Christ the Sacrament of the Encounter With God* (Kansas City: Sheed and Ward) 1963.

7. Many of the insights contained in this chapter come from the plenary discussion during "Toward a Lucan Spirituality," the general retreat of The Order of Saint Luke, October 17-21, 1994 held in Pittsburgh. My appreciation to all whose contributions are included above! - DWV

Two
Affirming the Apostolic Hope

This Jesus God raised up, and of that we are witnesses.

(Acts 2:32)

They devoted themselves to the teaching of the apostles.

(Acts 2:42a)

The apostolic hope is grounded in God's grace. By that grace we become new creatures, born anew through the resurrection of Jesus Christ from the dead. The transforming power of God's grace comes to us through the presence of the risen Christ, and that is what Christian worship is all about. As another New Testament writer proclaims:

> Blessed be the God and Father of our Lord Jesus Christ!
> By [God's] great mercy we have been born anew to a living
> hope through the resurrection of Jesus Christ from the dead,
> and to an inheritance which is imperishable, undefiled, and
> unfading, kept in heaven for you, who by God's power are
> guarded through faith for a salvation ready to be revealed
> in the last time.
>
> 1 Peter 1:3-5 (RSV alt)

Yves Congar insists that liturgy manifests the fullness of the Christian mystery and is the way in which the Church experiences over and over again the *paschal mystery*.[1] How are we to understand that phrase "the paschal mystery?" For James F. White,

> the paschal mystery is the risen Christ present and active
> in our worship. 'Mystery' in this sense is God's self-disclo-
> sure of that which passes human understanding or the
> revelation of that hitherto hidden. The 'paschal' element
> is the central, redemptive act of Christ in his life, minis-
> try, suffering, death, resurrection, and ascension.[2]

12

That broadens our unerstanding considerably from the old medieval focus on the crucifixion; yet our appropriation of the depth dynamic of the paschal mystery keeps expanding. The first chapter of John's gospel sets these crucial aspects of the paschal mystery in the context of both creation and incarnation. And, at the other "end," not only does it include Pentecost,[3] but also the final consummation. Centered in the death and resurrection of Jesus, the paschal mystery refers to our being incorporated into the whole saving act of Christ from creation to consummation.

Thus, the paschal mystery is not an *event* to which liturgy refers but *a reality present in the act of worship itself.* The apostolic hope reminds us that we are not involved in the celebration of past events as past. Rather, Christian liturgy focuses on key moments in salvation history as we appropriate them in the present. This orientation orients our *meaning sculpting* toward transformation into Christ — our ongoing formation as Christian disciples nourished by God's grace.

This concept of "meaning sculpting" grew out of a long and intense process which my wife and I shared during her preparation of a book manuscript. We were seeking a term which recognized that we do not merely "discover meaning," but rather that meaning is the result of a creative process. On the other hand, meaning is not created in a vacuum but must work with what is "given to us" or "discovered" through experience. "Sculpting" seems to take seriously both aspects.[4]

The Easter Vigil engages us in this kind of meaning sculpting. The key moments in salvation history are celebrated in the Service of the Word, culminating in the narrative of the resurrection. The service of the baptismal covenant, including our own baptismal renewal, focuses on our contemporary experience of God's saving love, and in the Eucharist we give thanks and share at Christ's table with a family to which we belong, and with whom we are commissioned to serve in the here and now. All of these components contribute to sculpting a deep experience of the apostolic hope.

One of the most powerful symbols of that hope is the *paschal candle*. In the service of light in the Easter vigil, its connection with the resurrection of Jesus Christ is clear. The light of Christ is the light that shines in our darkness and our darkness cannot overcome it. It shines throughout the great fifty days from Easter through Pentecost. It shines whenever there is a celebration of the baptismal covenant. It shines at Christian funerals. At all these times, it testifies to the paschal mystery which is at the heart of the apostolic hope, and thus the foundation of all Christian liturgy.

The sculpting of meaning which we experience in relation to liturgy also celebrates God as source of nourishment for our life pilgrimage. The basic questions we ask are interrelated. One of the answers to the question: "who am I?" comes when I find my place within a community. A community is bound together by the stories it tells. We discover our own identity in the resonance which occurs between those stories and our own lives.

In the great "Thanksgiving Over the Water" prayer of the Baptismal Covenant, the part of our common story having to do with water is recalled.[6] God's mighty acts are affirmed:

> — bringing forth light in the midst of chaos (creation)
> — saving those in the ark from the flood and
>   setting in the clouds a rainbow;
> — freeing the Israelites from slavery in Egypt
>   by leading them through the sea;
> — bringing their children through the Jordan to
>   the promised land;
> — nurturing Jesus in the water of a womb;
> — and anointing Jesus with the Spirit in his
>   baptism by John.

The recital of those mighty acts put us in touch with the story in a new context. For here the focus is on the water of baptism. It is possible for us to use the sign of water as a symbol to illuminate our own spiritual journey, and to be nourished by recalling the mighty acts of God in our own lives.

There have been times when chaos seemed ready to engulf us, but the light of God's grace sustained and empowered us. Interestingly, water is a symbol of both destruction and sustenance. It can overwhelm us, but without it we cannot live. The water of baptism reminds us that in the midst of the threat of destruction, God has acted in our lives to sustain us.

When the rains fell and the floods came, the ark became an instrument of salvation. In Christian symbolism, the ark has become a symbol for the Church. When we seem to be "at sea" in our lives, with *terra firma* nowhere in sight, the Church can keep us afloat. Within it are persons who have cared for us and shared our burdens and joys with us. But even more than that, it is the arena in which we are reminded of God's love and care even when we do not feel it. The rainbow tells us the sun is there, even if we cannot see it. In the water of baptism, there is a rainbow of hope which nourishes us, even as the ark of the Church keeps us from being drowned.

We have known slavery, too — slavery to old ideas, to preconditioned attitudes, to destructive habits, to oppressive forces beyond our control. However, we know that God is a liberating God, who acts to free us. The water of baptism is the sign that God has acted to free us from sin and death, and will act to liberate us from the oppressions which may still enslave us.

The way to freedom leads through the water. It was true for the Israelites, and it is true for us. We are called to go "through the Jordan" to the land of promise. Baptism recalls the past, affirms God's power in the present, and leads us into the future. As Thomas Clarke puts it:

> the sacrament of the present moment is like every sacrament — it is the sign of the already-real, the now-here presence of God, and at the same time a sign of the not-yet presence of God when the kingdom comes in its fullness.[6]

Spiritual pilgrimage is a matter of moving on. In the midst of the valley, we are encouraged to "keep on keeping on." The question of Wesley: "Are you going on to perfection?" must be answered anew every time we celebrate a baptism and renew our own baptismal covenant. We have not arrived; we are a people on the way.

Yet, we have been nurtured in the water of a womb, for the Holy Spirit is continually at work bringing us to new birth, and we are anointed with the Spirit in our baptism. Hands are laid upon us as these words are spoken:

> The Holy Spirit work within you, that being born through water and the Spirit you may be a faithful disciple of Jesus Christ.

Similar words are used at the renewal of our baptismal covenant, and may be used at any time when persons desire to reaffirm their faith, for "confirmation" is a repeatable act, available to us again and again.[7]

We are birthed to discipleship in the womb of the spirit. Birthing may be accompanied by pain, but it is always enabled by the nourishment we have already received. God's prevenient grace — the grace that goes before, nourishing, sustaining, and preparing us — enables us to respond to the claim of Christ upon our lives. The water of baptism reminds us of that spirit-womb which brings us to new life, anointed by the Spirit. As James White observes:

> Baptism is one of the chief means through which Christians perceive God's self-giving. It is an event received as pure gift; no one ever deserves baptism. . . . It is not something we do for ourselves; the self-giving is God's and the administration of it is another's.[8]

We appropriate baptism as a sacrament of identity as we hear the resonance between the affirmations of the Thanksgiving over the Water and our own lives. In addition, the prayers make reference to images of baptism in the New Testament which help us understand who we are.

Foremost among these is the understanding of baptism as dying and rising with Christ.[9] The relationship of baptism to the paschal mystery is clear near the end of the prayer when we pray:

> Pour out your Holy Spirit, to bless this gift of water and those who receive it . . . that, dying and being raised with Christ, they may share in his final victory.

What does it mean for us to die and be raised with Christ? To die with Christ involves our response to the invitation to "take up your cross daily and follow me" (Luke 9:23).[10] Our cross is not something which is thrust upon us, but something we choose to carry. A cross is costly to us; it demands our total commitment, for it is a symbol of life-and-death investment for us. Crosses are not borne to give evidence of our own righteousness, or to benefit ourselves. Taking up the cross is something we choose to do for the benefit of others at cost to ourselves.

In the process, we die to self-centeredness (although not to self-worth), to that tendency to see ourselves at the center of the universe. And we are raised to new life in Christ — a life lived in praise and thanksgiving to God and in love and service to others.

However, we must not lose sight of the understanding that our dying and rising is *with Christ*. Our life is "hid with Christ in God" (Colossians 3:3). Our baptism is our participation in the paschal mystery itself. As Paul writes:

> Do you not know that all of us who have been baptized into Christ Jesus were baptized into his death? We were buried therefore with him by baptism into death, so that as Christ was raised from the dead by the glory of the Father, we too might walk in newness of life. For if we have been united

16

> with him in a death like his, we shall certainly be united with
> him in a resurrection like his. (Romans 6:3-5)[11]

In the baptismal covenant we confront again the call to take up our cross daily, to have our lives hid with Christ in God, and to share in his death and resurrection.

We also find our identity in baptism as we pray: "wash away their sin and clothe them in righteousness."[12] Paul reminds us of this truth when he writes:

> We know that our old self was crucified with him so that
> the sinful body might be destroyed, and we might no longer
> be enslaved to sin. For those who have died are freed from
> sin. But if we have died with Christ, we believe that we
> shall also live with him. . . . So you also must consider
> yourselves dead to sin and alive to God in Christ Jesus.
> (Romans 6:6-8, 11)

In the baptismal covenant the forgiving and cleansing power of God is proclaimed.[13] The emphasis is not on repentance and the confession of our sins, although there will be times when we must hear that message if we are to die to sin and self-centeredness. Rather, the focus is on the power of the Holy Spirit to make us new creatures in Christ. Thus, our baptismal "garment" as it were, is to be clothed with Christ, having been cleansed of our sin. One of the most powerful assurances of forgiveness I experience is the affirmation: "Friends in Christ, we are a forgiven people!" That is the affirmation of the baptismal covenant.

As new creatures in Christ, cleansed from sin and empowered to live a resurrection life, we discover who we are and what we are called to become. The call to discipleship brings with it the gift of identity from the Christ who calls us. Call and response are brought together in the paschal mystery.

> May the God of hope fill [us] with all joy and peace in
> believing, so that by the power of the Holy Spirit, [we]
> may abound in hope.
>
> Romans 15:13 alt

Veni, Sancte Spiritus! Come, Holy Spirit, and empower us to affirm the apostolic hope, not only with our lips but in our lives!

17

Endnotes

1. A brief summary of the position of Yves Congar appears in Kevin W. Irwin, *Liturgical Theology: A Primer* (Collegeville, MN: The Liturgical Press, 1990) p. 19.

2. James F. White, *Introduction to Christian Worship* Rev. ed. (Nashville: Abingdon Press, 1990), p. 30. See also the position developed by Odo Casel in *The Mystery of Christian Worship* (Westminster: Newman, 1962).

3. Joyce Anne Zimmerman, *Liturgy as Living Faith: A Liturgical Spirituality* (Associated University Presses, 1993).

4. See Linda J. Vogel, *Teaching and Learning in Communities of Faith: Empowering Adults Through Religious Education* (San Francisco: Jossey-Bass, 1991), pp. 27-28.

5. All references to the liturgical text are taken from "The Baptismal Covenant I" in *The United Methodist Hymnal* (Nashville: The United Methodist Publishing House, 1989), pp. 33-39.

6. Thomas E. Clarke, S.J. "Never a Dull Moment," in *Weavings*, Vol. II, Number 3 (May/June, 1987), p. 19.

7. See the exposition of this understanding of confirmation in Robert L. Browning and Roy A. Reed, *The Sacraments in Religious Education and Liturgy* (Birmingham, AL: Religious Education Press, 1985), chapter 10, pp. 191-202. For a more complete development, see Browning and Reed's book, *Models of Confirmation and Baptismal Affirmation* (Birmingham, AL: Religious Education Press, 1995), especially Part I.

8. James F. White, *Sacraments as God's Self-Giving* (Nashville: Abingdon Press, 1983), p. 34. On baptism as a celebration of new birth, cf. p. 41.

9. For example, see Romans 6:3-5 and Colossians 2:21. For a discussion of baptism as union to Jesus Christ and his work, see James F. White, *Sacraments as God's Self-Giving*, pp. 36-37.

10. See also Matthew 10:38 and 16:24, Mark 8:34, Luke 14:27 and 23:26. On baptism into the death of Christ, see Tad Guzie, *The Book of Sacramental Basics* (New York: Paulist Press, 1981), pp. 76-77.

11. For insight into the relationship of baptism with the transformation of the "spiritual body," see Gustavo Gutierrez, *We Drink From Our Own Wells* (Maryknoll, N.Y.: Orbis Books, 1984), pp. 66-67.

12. For example, see I Corinthians 6:11 and Galatians 3:27.

13. For an insightful discussion of baptism as the assurance of forgiveness and the priority of "original love" over "original sin," see Tad Guzie, *The Book of Sacramental Basics*, pp. 81-86.

Three

Being the Church of Jesus Christ

They devoted themselves to . . . the koinonia.

(Acts 2:42b)

The paschal mystery is, by its very nature, *ecclesial*; that is, the death and resurrection of Jesus has to do, not just with Jesus of Nazareth, but with the community of those who live that death and resurrection into the future.[1] That community — which we call the Church — rehearses, celebrates, and is transformed by the liturgy. Further, Alexander Schmemann observes:

> If liturgical theology stems from an understanding of worship as the public act of the Church, then its final goal will be to clarify and explain the connection between this act and the Church, i.e. to explain how the Church expresses and fulfills herself in this act.[2]

Liturgy as ecclesial act

We use the word "liturgy" today to talk about "the public worship of the Church."[3] Behind that meaning, however, lies a deep truth:

> In classical Greek, liturgy (*leitourgia*) had a secular meaning; it denoted a work (*érgon*) undertaken on behalf of the people (*laos*). Public projects undertaken for the good of the community . . . would be called *leitourgia*.[4]

Thus, we can speak of liturgy as "the work of the people." I. H. Dalmais rightly concludes that liturgy is "ecclesial event."[5] What is the nature of that event? What does it tell us about who the Church is? What does it have to do with the meaning and nourishment we seek?

Yves Congar insists that as the Church praises God, a "holy communion" with God through Christ is engendered.[6] The nature of this communion reminds us that a dialogical understanding of the Church is crucial. Over-emphasis upon what God does can lead to a *docetic* view of the Church, treating churches as though they fully manifested the perfection of divine community, which we know they do not. Over-emphasis upon what people do denies the Biblical understanding of the Church as *ecclesia*, the called-out community which responds to the initiative of God's grace.[7]

Thus for Alexander Schmemann, worship constitutes the Church by transforming private and subjective experience into a new life which is "shared with all in Christ" and thus belongs to the body rather than being restricted to the individual. Christian worship is the expression of the Church "as the unity of that Body whose Head is Christ," serving God "with one mouth and one heart."[8]

Christian worship, however, cannot do this as an in-group asserting the exclusivity of its corporate identity. Rather, as Peter Fink observes, worship is a "moment of invitation . . . when all that the Church understands about itself is celebrated in order to invite people more deeply into the mystery."[9]

This corporate action resonates with our individual pilgrimage. The liturgy expresses faith through word and symbol. These word/symbol/events recall and re-member the faith of the Church so that we may sculpt meaning and receive nourishment as individuals in community and as a community which is more than a collection of individuals. The sacraments help us understand that reality.

Baptism: A Sacrament of Belonging

To be a human being is to live in community. As infants, we cannot fend for ourselves. We are dependent on other persons or we will not survive. The quality of relationships which we experience in those early years molds our capacity to receive from beyond ourselves with gratitude. Our spirituality does not grow in a vacuum, either. We do not invent worship and prayer. We experience them in Christian community before we are even aware of what is happening.

We do not choose the family or faith community into which we are born. Yet it makes a very real difference in our lives. The same thing is true with our citizenship, the analogy I have found most helpful in pre-baptismal counseling.

A child is born the citizen of a certain nation. She did nothing positively or negatively to merit it; it is totally undeserved. And yet, it has crucial implications. In some instances, it may mean inadequate nutrition, a restricted life-expectancy, or circumscribed freedoms. In others, it spells opportunity and possibility and liberty. Those potentials come to the child as a gift, for good or ill.

A child who is born or adopted by believing parents within a faith community receives a gift. It is not merited or deserved; it is sheer grace. But it makes a very real difference. Hearing the Story, listening to the songs, experiencing the prayers nourish a child within the community of faith. Growing up within the Church provides a person with sources of spiritual nourishment.

However, receiving the gift does not mean that one is constrained to make use of it. People handle the gift of their citizenship in different ways. Some reject it and opt for some other loyalty. Most of us know of persons in our family tree who rejected the citizenship of the "old country" in order to become a citizen of this country.

The same thing may happen to our Christian citizenship. One may reject it, and opt for some other world religion (such as Buddhism or Islam), or some secular religion (such as materialism, either of the capitalist or Marxist variety). Being born into the faith community does not preclude the possibility of rejection.

The number of those who make such a conscious rejection of their citizenship or their Christianity may be relatively few. There are many more who take it for granted, but do as little as possible with it.

In terms of citizenship, that may mean paying taxes but not voting or keeping informed about public policy issues. In the life of the Church, we may speak of these persons as the "lapsed baptized" — the potential for nourishment was there but was never actualized. Some of these persons are in what has been called the "hatched, matched, and dispatched" crowd — they come to Church to be baptized, married, and buried. Others may put in their appearance in connection with festivals such as Christmas and Easter which evoke nostalgic memories. Such persons do not live out their baptism, but keep the connection alive — just barely, it may be true. Sometimes that is enough, and new life can be manifested when situations force us back on resources beyond ourselves and we discover there is more to our religious heritage than we supposed. But what we hope for is the living out of our citizenship, whether in the nation or within the reign

21

and the rule of God. Living out our baptism is a matter of "becoming who we are."[10]

The context for our spiritual pilgrimage of becoming is that of the Christian community. If we listen carefully to what we say when we celebrate the baptismal covenant, that communal context becomes quite apparent. The first words of The Baptismal Covenant service reaffirm that our place of belonging is within the community of faith we call the Church:[11]

> Brothers and sisters in Christ:
> Through the Sacrament of Baptism, believers and their
>   households are initiated into Christ's holy Church.

When all candidates have been baptized, we affirm together:

> "With joy and thanksgiving we welcome you
> as members of the family of Christ."

The answer to the question "where do I belong?" is "within the community of God's people bound together by the grace of our Lord, Jesus Christ." Baptism is a gift of the Holy Spirit which marks us as living in a faith community empowered by the Spirit's presence.[12] We are not on our pilgrimage alone. While each of us is an unique individual, we are a part of the body of Christ.

There are times when we feel very much alone. Like Elijah, I may think I am the only faithful person around (I Kings 19:9-18). The Baptismal Covenant reminds me that I am part of a great community of those who sought to be faithful, a community both past and present. We need to tell our corporate stories, and ground ourselves in the Biblical heritage we share.

> Therefore, since we are surrounded by so great a cloud of
> witnesses, let us also lay aside every weight, and sin which
> clings so closely, and let us run with perseverance the race
> that is set before us, looking to Jesus the pioneer and per-
> fecter of our faith, who for the joy that was set before him
> endured the cross, despising the shame, and is seated at
> the right hand of the throne of God. (Hebrews 12:1-2)

In baptism we celebrate the "belonging" which results from being a part of the Church, Christ's body on earth.[13] This is spelled out in reflection on the word-event of the Eucharist called to mind by the words:

The Body of Christ Given for You

We start with the recognition that the body of Christ is given. It is an experience of grace, the gifting of our lives by God. What we take and eat is always given to us.

The body of Christ given to us is focused first and foremost in the gift of Jesus Christ himself. The body of Christ reminds us of the incarnation — the Word made flesh who came to dwell among us, full of grace and truth. He reconciled us to God through the death of his body on the cross (Ephesians 2:14-16), and was raised on the third day. The body of Christ given for us is the incarnate, living, suffering, dying, risen Lord. To focus on any one aspect of that gift to the total exclusion of others impoverishes us.

In one sense, this gift may be located in the history of the first century. If that were all, remembering the past might be an adequate response. However, the New Testament writers are convinced that Christ is risen.[14] The presence of Christ is not just a gift in the past, but a present reality and a hope for the future. So, as we proclaim the mystery of faith we affirm:

"Christ has died, Christ is risen, Christ will come again!"[15]

When we receive the gift of the bread and the cup, we receive the body of Christ — crucified, risen, coming — and thereby become what we are called to be: the body of Christ, the Church.

It is significant that these gifts come to us out of the natural world for, in the words of Theodore Runyon, the world is itself the "original sacrament."[16] What we eat and drink, the air we breathe, the clothing we wear, the places in which we live and work and worship, all come from the world which is given to us.

Bread and wine are rich symbols of our understanding of the grace of God in our lives. However, when they are presented they bear the marks of the works of our hands. They have been cultivated, harvested, and processed by human beings. As such they are symbols of our stewardship of all that is given to us.

When Jesus took the bread and the cup at the last supper and said, "This is my body which is given for you" and "this is my blood of the new covenant," he was taking what had been given by God, received and acted upon by human labor, lifted up for blessing by God, and offered back again as a new reality.

In that sequence we find a recapitulation of our lives and of the life of the Church: All is given us by God, and the way in which we use it is a mark of our stewardship. When we offer it back to God, it is blessed in a new way, and we receive it back again transformed, with new meaning and with greater capacity to nourish and sustain us. What is true for the whole life of the Church is made transparent in the celebration of the Eucharist.

The focus of that gift again returns to Jesus Christ, for he is the One who offers up those natural, yet human-wrought realities to be transformed by God. What we are given is food indeed, and drink indeed, but it is clear that it is not meant primarily to meet our need for physical nourishment. Rather, it is sign and symbol of all the nourishment God gives us — through world and Word, through font and table, through prayer and pilgrimage.

In it we find yet a third layer of meaning revealed. For the body of Christ given for us is also to be found in the gift of the Church. We make the context for receiving communion clear at the time of the breaking of bread (what is called the *fraction*) when we say:

> Because there is one loaf, we, who are many, are one body,
> for we all partake of the one loaf. The bread which we break
> is a sharing in the body of Christ.

The Church is a gift given to us. We are members one of another. Christian worship, when it is vital, is an "epiphany" — a "showing forth" or "manifesting" of the Church. As our worship enables us to enter into salvation history, we become the *ecclesia* — the Church as a called-out people, becoming who we are, aware of our corporate nature, and able to speak and act out of that reality.

A Lukan liturgical spirituality is ecclesial. *Veni, Sancte Spiritus!* Come, Holy Spirit, and empower us to live out our identity as members of the Body of Christ, the Church!

Endnotes

1. Cf. I. H. Dalmais, *Introduction to the Liturgy*, trans. Roger Capel (Baltimore: Helicon, 1961), p. 40. The perspective of "remembering the future" comes from Letty Russell in *Household of Freedom* (Philadelphia: Westminster Press, 1987).

2. Alexander Schmemann, *Introduction to Liturgical Theology* (Crestwood, NY: St. Vladimir's Seminary Press, 1986), p. 17.

3. Lawrence J. Madden, "Liturgy" in Peter Fink, ed., *The New Dictionary of Sacramental Basics* (Collegeville, MN: Liturgical Press, 1990) p. 740.

4. Ibid.

5. Dalmais, ibid.

6. Yves Congar, *Tradition and Traditions*, Miachael Naseby and Thomas Rainborough, trans. (New York: Macmillan, 1966), p. 427.

7. Dalmais goes so far as to differentiate between liturgical and sacramental theology in preserving both poles. For him, sacramental theology has to do with what God, in and through "acts of salvation," does for the Church. On the other hand, liturgical theology deals with what Church does as it engages in acts of worship (see Dalmais, *ibid.*, p. 66). Such a distinction may seem to make a clean and helpful distinction, but scholarly consensus is that it will not hold up. Liturgical theology cannot understand the action of the Church without reference to what God does to birth and sustain it. Sacramental theology has to recognize that sacraments are sign-acts of the Church as it worships. While those sign-acts are based upon God's grace, they are also liturgy, the work of the people, or to be more exact, the public work of the people.

8. Alexander Schmemann, *Introduction to Liturgical Theology* (Crestwood, NY: St. Vladimir's Seminary Press, 1986), p. 24.

9. Peter Fink, "Towards a Liturgical Theology" in *Worship* 47 (December, 1973), p. 602.

10. Soren Kierkegaard was more concerned about "becoming Christian" than he was about "being Christian." The distinction is helpful, although I would make the case that "being Christian" is itself a mode of becoming. See also William H. Willimon, *Remember Who You Are; Baptism: A Model for Christian Life* (Nashville: Upper Room, 1980).

11. All references to the liturgical text are taken from "The Baptismal Covenant I" in *The United Methodist Hymnal* (Nashville: The United Methodist Publishing House, 1989), pp. 33-39.

12. See James F. White, *Sacraments as God's Self-Giving* (Nashville: Abingdon Press, 1983), pp. 38-39.
13. Ibid, pp. 37-38.
14. For example, see Acts 17:3, Romans 8:34, I Corinthians 15.
15. Unless otherwise noted, references to the eucharistic liturgy are taken from *The United Methodist Book of Worship* (Nashville: The United Methodist Publishing House, 1992). In earlier work in this area, I refer to *Holy Communion: A Service Book for Use by the Minister*, Supplemental Worship Resources 16 (Nashville: Abingdon Press, 1987) and *The Book of Services* (Nashville: The United Methodist Publishing House, 1985). Cf. also *The United Methodist Hymnal; Book of United Methodist Worship* (Nashville: The United Methodist Publishing House, 1989), pp. 6-11.
16. See the summary in Browning and Reed, *The Sacraments in Religious Education and Liturgy* (op. cit.), pp. 31-32. For a more complete treatment, see Theodore Runyon, "The World as Original Sacrament," *Worship* 54 (1980), pp. 495-511.

Four

Magnifying the Sacraments

They devoted themselves . . . to the breaking of bread.

(Acts 2:42c)

In the last chapter we noted that celebrating the Eucharist helps us understand the Church as the Body of Christ, and in a later chapter we will explore how appropriating the deeply dynamic dimensions of the Baptismal Covenant can enable us to live a sacramental life. Baptism and Eucharist have been important parts of the Church's life since the days of the early Church, as a careful reading of the Acts of the Apostles makes clear.

Nevertheless, a study of the history of Christian worship reveals that the way in which the sacraments have been understood and appropriated is amazingly diverse.[1] Turning to the contemporary situation, we become aware that, with the exception of Anglican and Lutheran traditions, the role of the sacraments in many Protestant denominations is more marginal than one might expect.

"Magnifying the sacraments" may seem like strange language at first. After all, it is the sacraments which should nourish and form us. The sacraments magnify God's grace in Jesus Christ, and as central acts of the Church at worship they should undergird our doing and our being as Christians.

But what *ought* to be the case and what *is* in fact the case are not congruent! A Lukan approach to liturgical spirituality and the sacramental life demands that we give time and attention to reclaiming the role of the sacraments as essential to the life of the corporate Church and to the pilgrimage of faith for those who seek to follow Jesus.

Talking about the meaning of the word "sacrament" is apt to be confusing. The word *sacramentum* is not a New Testament word at all but a Latin term used to translate the Greek *mysterion*, and the two terms are not at all equivalent. Rather than talk about the historical process by

27

which all of this took place, however, let us look at how we use the word today.[2]

Foundational Sacraments

There are three ways in which word "sacrament" has been used which may seem surprising. These uses do not have to do with the "traditional" sacraments of Protestant, Roman Catholic, or Eastern Orthodox Churches. I call them "foundational sacraments" because they help me understand what undergirds not only baptism and eucharist but sacramental living in general.

I begin by reflecting on Theodore Runyon's observation that the world is the "original sacrament."[3] Implicit is a recognition that creation is itself an act of grace, that the creation is essentially good and not evil, and that through the creation we can glimpse the Transcendent. As I write this chapter, I am surrounded by the beauty of the mountains of western South Dakota. The wind in the pines and the rushing stream across the road can be heard through the open window. A spring sparkles cold and clear behind our cabin, and we see deer and elk and antelope on early morning drives. On clear nights, when there is no human light in sight, we can gaze into the glory of the heavens.

Now none of these sights and sounds are sacramental in and of themselves. Indeed, for some they are not sacramental at all because there is no wonder in them, and for others, they are not sacramental because in and of themselves they become the objects of worship. But for me — not always, but on more than a few occasions — the veil is torn away, the aperture is opened, and I become filled with awe for the Transcendent One who is above all, and through all, and in all.[4] So called "primitive peoples" without the benefit of revealed theology often have this sense in deep and profound ways.

It is out of this innate goodness of creation, and the potential of creation to carry a sense of that which is beyond it, that water and oil and bread and wine can be seen as "vehicles of grace"— elements whose significance is profound for those who look with the eyes of faith. So Paul Tillich writes:

> The universal religious basis is the experience of the Holy within the finite. Universally in everything finite and particular, or in this and that finite, the Holy appears in a

28

special way. I could call this the sacramental basis of all religions — the holy here and now which can be seen, heard, dealt with, in spite of its mysterious character.[5]

If the world is the "original sacrament" of God's grace, Edward Schillebeeckx makes it clear that "the man Jesus, as the personal visible realization of the divine grace of redemption, is *the* sacrament, the primordial sacrament."[6] We recall the importance of the paschal mystery in our discussion of the apostolic hope. Christian sacramental living needs to be based in this fundamental recognition of Jesus as the primordial sacrament of God's grace for us. Indeed, it is because of that sense, however expressed, that the man Jesus of Nazareth becomes Jesus the Christ, Jesus the Lord, Jesus the Child of God.

The third of these "foundational sacraments," as I have chosen to call them, is the Church itself as a sacrament of salvation. As Edward Schillebeeckx affirms:

> What God's grace, [God's] absolute, gratuitous and forgiving proximity has already begun to do in the lives of all [persons] becomes an *epiphany* in the Church. . . . The Church is the primordial sacrament of the salvation of all . . . .[7]

It is a sacrament of salvation because it is also a sacrament of God's grace and a sacrament of Christ's presence. A depth understanding of the Church as the Body of Christ (in which Christ's real presence is in the *koinonia*) is inherently sacramental, whether or not it is specifically articulated.

Karl Rahner ties all three perspectives together:

> Sacraments point not just to *things* through which the Holy can be revealed. Rather, all of nature and history reveal the cosmic grace of God to which the individual sacraments are witnesses and expressions. God's grace is bringing wholeness and salvation at the roots of human experience. . . . God's cosmic, essential grace is visible in many ways, but supremely in Jesus Christ, the primordial sacrament, and in the Church, the presently *visible*, ministering, caring, serving body of Christ.[8]

Creation, Jesus and the Church are foundational theologically, for an implicit or explicit recognition of their sacramentality undergirds depth understandings of the sacramental acts of the Church. But they are not foundational historically or liturgically. It is not magnifying *sacramentality* which is our concern in this chapter; it is magnifying the sacraments of the Church. We can find a way to tie these basic or foundational sacraments to the sacraments of the Church in James White's affirmation that God's self-giving is the basis of the Christian sacraments. . . . God gives us sacraments as a continual means of manifesting God's love for us.[9]

Sacraments of the Church

The two central sacraments of the Church have been, and continue to be, Baptism and Eucharist. I will follow my own tradition in focusing on these two, while recognizing that at some times and in some traditions, other acts of the Church have also been seen as sacraments. Indeed, I would insist that much of what the Church does is sacramental in nature, and that those actions will be enriched if they are seen in relation to the Baptismal Covenant and the Eucharistic Meal. Such a perspective will be an on-going theme in this book.

In magnifying *the* sacraments, however, it is Baptism and Eucharist to which we will give our attention. Both are means of grace through which we are incorporated into the paschal mystery. They interpret each other. Together they form us as the Body of Christ, the real presence of Christ in the world, and help us understand our identity and our mission.

For Alexander Schmemann, the Eucharist is "*the* sacrament of the Church, i.e. her eternal actualization as the Body of Christ, united in Christ by the Holy Spirit."[10] It is relationship with the risen Christ which is at stake, as Edward Schillebeeckx makes clear:

> [The Eucharist] takes the form of a commemorative meal in which the usual secular significance of the bread and wine is withdrawn and these become bearers of Christ's gift of himself — 'take and eat, this is my body.' Christ's gift of himself, however, is not ultimately directed toward bread and wine, but toward the faithful. . . . In this commemorative meal, bread and wine become the subject of a new *establishment of meaning*, not by [human beings] but by

the living Lord *in* the Church, through which they become
the sign of the real presence of Christ giving himself to
us.[11]

The Baptismal Covenant is also at the heart of a Lukan approach to
liturgical spirituality and the sacramental life. We will explore the nature
of that covenant later, but here we want to note that

> Christian baptism is rooted in the ministry of Jesus of
> Nazareth, in his death and in his resurrection. It is incor-
> poration into Christ, who is the crucified and risen Lord;
> it is entry into the New Covenant between God and God's
> people.[12]

If we accept the importance of the Eucharist and the Baptismal Covenant to the life of the Church as well as to the pilgrimage of faith, how
can we help the congregation of which we are a part share in that reality?

I believe we need to start with an insistence that the celebration of
the sacraments is not tangential to the life of the Church but at its very
center. Our work in this area must be first and foremost *relational*. Celebration of the sacraments involves people — our brothers and sisters in
Jesus Christ. Their experiences and values must be taken into account.
Magnifying the sacraments has to do with people, not just manipulating
liturgical rites. Because the Church is *koinonia*, it must take relationshipts
seriously. This does not mean trying to please everyone all the time, or
being held hostage by a vocal minority. It does mean trying to understand
what is at stake for other persons, taking context and local tradition seriously, honoring the deepest and richest experiences of sacramentality out
of which we can work.

Another implication is that magnifying the sacraments is something
for clergy and laity to do together. The importance of the sacraments is
not something for clergy to foist upon laity without their support, nor are
the sacraments to be seen as the possession of those entrusted with their
celebration. The chief celebrants in any Eucharist or Baptismal Covenant
service are not the "pastors" but the priests — and here I refer *to the priesthood of all believers*. All are celebrants; all are liturgists; all are priests. The
presider does so on behalf of and for the sake of the whole assembly.

When one undertakes this work, whether as clergy or laity, one must
be aware that one can be wrong even when one is doing things "right."
That is, if the community is torn apart rather than being built up, liturgical correctness is of little value.

Strategizing the work of building up a sense of the importance of the sacraments involves knowing what one would like to have happen, how often, and in what way. If I had only my own values and understandings to consider, how would these celebrations take place? Having worked that out in my own mind (and recognizing that I am still growing and will likely change my mind!), I must then assess what is the most helpful thing to do in this particular context. This always involves some prioritizing. Are there some things which are non-negotiable? These are the things for which I would rather leave this congregation (whether as pastor or parishioner) rather than change. I believe the list of such things should be quite small, and even there, I should be open to the teaching of the Holy Spirit broadening my horizons as to what is truly important. But there will probably be some such things, and it will be better if I know what they are, although I don't broadcast the list!

Often there is considerable difference between what is and what I wish it were. I must then assess what changes can take place soon because others will be open to them; what changes will take time and education but may be possible; and which changes are unlikely ever to be productive and spiritually beneficial in this particular context. Alongside these, I must place the practices which are now taking place which I want to nurture, honor, and support. Some of these may be "transportable" to other settings; some will be unique to this setting. My own experience is that the longer I am in a particular congregation, the more I am surprised by the things which move from the "to-be-changed" list to the "to-be-kept-and-honored" list. What happens is that the Spirit gradually teaches me the deep meaning of practices which may at first seem superficial or inadequate. One must keep open even as one seeks growth in a congregation's sense of the sacraments.

Education and nurture are key ingredients to this growth. Across the age span, from young children to shut-ins and elders, we must seek ways to make the sacraments vital and significant for people and to help them reflect on their meaning for the life of faith and the nature of the Church. Teaching about the sacraments whenever and where-ever possible is a key strategy.

Whether in teaching or preaching, one becomes increasingly sensitive to ways in which the Baptismal Covenant and the Eucharist provide images and illustrations of what Christian discipleship is all about. Gradually our thinking about discipleship and the nature of the Church become permeated with sacramental motifs.

The celebration of the sacraments themselves must be approached with care. On the one hand, we seek services which have Biblical, theological, and liturgical integrity. On the other hand, we want these services to be vital and alive, engaging us all in the grace and love and joy God is ready to pour out upon us. Thus we will take the rituals which have been carefully prepared by our denominational tradition seriously. We will get to know them inside-out — that is, to get beneath the surface and discover the dynamic which drives them. We will read about and study and experience them until they become part of our inner being.

But we will not be held in bondage by them. By learning their depth dynamic we will have the freedom to know when to depart from them, when and how to modify them, when to utilize the wider ecumenical resources available. We will resist the temptation to "do our own thing" without regard to the tradition. When we depart from what is provided, we will know why. When we use what is provided, we will do so with all the vitality and strength the Tradition deserves if it is to remain alive and relevant.

We will seek opportunities for celebrating Eucharist and the Baptismal Covenant. In most congregations this will mean celebrating the Sacraments with greater frequency; sometimes, however, it may mean gathering individual events such as baptisms together so that they may have greater power and significance. In addition, we will seek to relate the Sacraments to important times and transition points in the lives of individuals and congregations.

We will pay particular attention to the interaction of the sacraments with the senses. We will always have a "fair linen" (even if it is only the size of a napkin) beneath the elements to remind us that this is a meal; the whiteness of the cloth signifying that the foundation of the Eucharist is God's grace. We will pour the water for the Baptismal Covenant so that it can be seen and heard. In whatever ways possible, we will focus attention on one loaf and a shared cup. We will let the "breaking of the bread" (the *fraction*) speak with integrity about the nature of the Church as the body of Christ. We will seek to use the paschal candle when it is appropriate. We will avoid "cluttering" the holy space with too many things to distract us from the central symbols. Such, at least, is a part of my list!

Central to all that we do will be the clear intention that our goal is to provide for ourselves and others an increased openness to the nurture, strength, and understanding which the sacraments provide. We magnify the sacraments not in order to worship them, but in order that through them, we may worship the living God of grace who comes to us in Jesus Christ.

Becoming sacraments of Sacraments of *The* Sacrament

Finally, you see, we are not only concerned with remembering Jesus' own prayer of thanksgiving at the Last Supper, or even offering up a Great Thanksgiving Prayer at the holy meal. What we discover is that the power of God is at work within us, teaching us to live all of life eucharistically, that is, in the framework of thanksgiving,[13] and to understand our discipleship as a living out of the Baptismal Covenant. We are to live as those who find their identity through lifting up our hearts — indeed our very lives — to God.[14]

It becomes natural for us to give thanks and praise to God in everything (see Philippians 4:6), to present ourselves "as a living sacrifice, holy and acceptable to God" (Romans 12:1).

We become a people upon whom the Holy Spirit is poured out with power to enable our ministry in Christ's name.

The sacraments reveal a dynamic basic to life itself for they involve both grace and faith. Indeed, the unity of relationship recognizes both the grace of God and the sign-acts of a faith community. Having offered all that we have and are up to God, we receive it all back again renewed and empowered. In all of life, we take and eat with thanksgiving, being nourished so that we can become the people we are called to be.

Veni, Sancte Spiritus! Come, Holy Spirit; make yourself known in and to and through us as we celebrate the holy sacraments of Christ's Church!

Endnotes

1. For example, see Herman Wegman, *Christian Worship in East and West: A Guide to Liturgical History* (Collegeville, MN: Pueblo, 1985).
2. Readers are encouraged to read the extremely helpful chapter in Browning and Reed, *The Sacraments in Religious Education and Liturgy* (op. cit.) where this process is described and the implications for our understanding drawn. See especially pp. 26-64.
3. Theodore Runyon, "The World as the Original Sacrament," *Worship* 54 (1980), pp. 495-511.
4. See Ephesians 4:6. The theological nature of this perspective is explored by W. Paul Jones in *Theological Worlds* (Nashville: Abingdon Press, 1989), pp. 11-121.
5. Paul Tillich, in *The Future of Religions*, Jerald C. Brauer ed. (New York: Harper and Row, 1966), p. 87.
6. Edward Schillebeeckx, *Christ the Sacrament of the Encounter with God* (New York: Sheed & Ward, 1963), p. 15.
7. Edward Schillebeeckx, *The Mission of the Church* (New York: Seabury Press, 1973), p. 17.
8. Karl Rahner, as summarized by Robert L. Browning and Roy A. Reed, *The Sacraments in Religious Education and Liturgy* (Birmingham, AL: Religious Education Press, 1985), p. 11.
9. James F. White, *Sacraments as God's Self Giving* (Nashville: Abingdon Press, 1983), pp. 13, 23.
10. Alexander Schmemann, *Introduction to Liturgical Theology* (Crestwood, NY: St. Vladimir's Seminary Press, 1986), p. 24.
11. Edward Schillebeeckx, *The Eucharist* (New York: Sheed and Ward, 1968), p. 151.
12. *Baptism, Eucharist and Ministry*, (Geneva: World Council of Churches, Faith and Order Paper No. 111, 1982) p. 2.
13. See Don E. Saliers, *Worship and Spirituality*, Revised ed. (Akron, Ohio: OSL Publications, 1996), chapter five, especially pages 62-68.
14. For a significant and stimulating study of the way in which the Wesleys understood the Eucharist, see J. Ernest Rattenbury, *The Eucharistic Hymns of John and Charles Wesley*, Second American ed. (Akron, OH: OSL Publications, 1996).

Five

Living the Sacramental Life

Yet [God] is not far from each one of us,
for in [God] we live and move and have our being.
(Acts 17:27b-28a)

If we affirm the apostolic hope, endeavor to live for the Church of Jesus Christ, and seek to magnify the sacraments, the natural result will be a commitment to live the sacramental life. Talking about "living the sacramental life" is a way of reflecting on sacramental spirituality. It takes place at the intersection of spirituality, liturgy, theologizing and praxis. Sacramental living defies compartmentalization; it is dynamic and holistic.

Sacramental spirituality emerges out of a sense of the holiness of the whole creation. All that has been created may become an icon of the Transcendent for us, opening us up to that which is beyond us and yet within us. We may find ourselves addressed by God in the majesty of the mountains and the beauty of the sunrise. But we also encounter God in the common things of life: water, bread, a cup which is shared. Nor is this transparency restricted to positive experiences. In the rape of the earth, the murder of the innocents, the oppression of the poor, and the arrogance of the powerful, we may encounter the God who suffers with and on behalf of a creation tainted by misuse.

Sacramental spirituality is centered in the paschal mystery. In the incarnation, life, death and resurrection of Jesus Christ, we have already seen that we encounter what Schillebeeckx calls "the primordial sacrament."[1] Jesus Christ is the sacrament of the presence of God, the sign and seal of God's extravagant grace. Baptism and Eucharist are grounded in the paschal mystery. So is daily prayer, the liturgical year, and the Pauline understanding of the Church as the body of Christ. The call to "take up our cross and follow" is a call to live within the paschal mystery and out of its life-embracing affirmation in the face of the death-dealing forces we encounter.

36

In this, we are not alone. Not only is God with us, but sacramental spirituality is a pilgrimage of individuals-in-community. If Christ is the sacrament of the presence of God, the Church is the sacrament of the living presence of the risen Christ. We are members one of another. Each of us brings gifts which no one else has in the same way. No one has all the gifts, and every gift is important to the body. Martin Buber observed that "all real living is meeting."[2] As individuals-in-community, we learn to value one another as kin – brothers and sisters with God-given worth who are our companions on our journey. Literally, companions are those with whom (*com*) we share bread (*pan*)! We are part of the *kin-dom* of God.

Sacramental spirituality means living out our baptism through the discipleship we share as companions. We have been washed in the waters of God's grace, marked by the cross of Christ, and anointed by the Holy Spirit. Every day we have the mandate and the opportunity to live out the implications of that reality. There is no corner of life in which our baptism is irrelevant. As my colleague Ruth Duck puts it, we are "water-washed and spirit-born."[3] Our baptism is the celebration of God's grace at work in our lives and our "ordination" to ministry in Christ's name.

Sacramental spirituality expresses itself in living eucharistically. We recall again that Alexander Schmemann speaks of human beings as *homo adorans*.[4] That is, the mark of our humanity is our capacity for worship. We receive all that we have and are as a gift. We stand as priests offering it all up to God. The miracle is that God gives it back to us again, transfigured, transformed, to be used in eucharistic living. Living eucharistically means living out of the context of this sense of giftedness and blessing. Pierre Teilhard de Chardin knew that the whole earth is the bread we offer, the suffering of all people, the wine we share.[5] Gratitude and interconnectedness intersect in eucharistic living. We receive the world from God and offer it to God, and by filling the world with this Eucharist, we transform our lives which we receive from the world into life in God. Such action is most transparent in vital worship: the praise of the living God, the celebration and living out of the sacraments.

Sacramental spirituality is not only concerned with a life of "personal holiness." Living our baptism with a eucharistic perspective necessarily involves us in social holiness as well. Concern for peace and justice, care for the oppressed, and opposition to the forces which dehumanize our neighbors are not options we can take or leave in living sacramentally. As the Church, we are the sacrament of God's presence, the living embodiment of the risen Christ for the sake of the world. We cannot do everything.

We are not all called to live out social justice in the same way. But we must wrestle with the implications of the gospel for the pain of the world, and be willing to follow Christ even into sacred precincts when there are tables which need turning over!

In all of this we must recognize that sacramental spirituality is the gracious work of the Holy Spirit. So often we try to separate our work and the work of the Spirit as if they were separate things (which only shows we do not understand either ourselves *or* the Spirit!).

As D. M. Baille first taught me in his classic *God Was In Christ*, there is a profound paradox in God's economy.[6] The clue is found in the deepest relationships we know. Love always comes as a gift; there is no way to earn it or merit it; in it we are always surprised by joy. But it is also true that love is the deep expression of our most profound and far-reaching commitment. In it we give ourselves from the very depth of our being to another.

That's how it is with the work of the Holy Spirit in our sacramental living: a sense of the holiness of all the world, of our interconnectedness with it, of the paschal mystery at work within us, of our companionship with other pilgrims, of a eucharistic dimension in the living out of our baptism, and of our mission in this hurting world — a sense of all that comes as a gift of the Spirit. It is too deep, too comprehensive, too profound for our limited capacity.

And yet, we know that we cannot just relax and see if it will happen. Our spirituality must be lived out in praxis — that vital dialogue between reflection and practice. Doing flows out of our being, and our being is grounded with Christ in God through the Holy Spirit. Thus, we find ourselves to be "stewards of the mysteries of God" (I Corinthians 4:1), and com-panions on the journey of sacramental living.

We will focus on three of the many areas through which we may seek to live the sacramental life. In this chapter, we will look at the Daily Office as a way of living sacramentally. In succeeding chapters, we will turn our attention to baptismal spirituality and the spirituality of the pastoral offices. These are intended to serve as examples, although very important ones, of ways in which we can reflect on the life of faith as a sacramental activity.

A Sacramental Sense of Time: The Daily Office

The Daily Office refers to a historic pattern of daily prayer in the life of the Church which identified certain times or "hours" for prayer; thus it has also been called "the liturgy of the hours." An *office* is a task or responsibility with which we are entrusted; the responsibility here is to fulfill the Church's task of prayer on behalf of the Church day by day.

In his classic work *The Shape of the Liturgy*, Dom Gregory Dix understands the Daily Office as a way of sanctifying time. It is a "liturgy of time,"[7] to be sure, but we will not want to separate "sanctified time" from the "eschatological Eucharist" or from baptismal spirituality. All are bound together in a liturgical spirituality.

Robert Taft, in his seminal work on liturgical theology and the Daily Office,[8] insists that the Daily Office is a window on the presence of the holy in all time — past, present, and future. The various offices are ritual moments signifying the whole of time.[9] In the Daily Office, the stories of salvation history from the past, the action of the Holy Spirit in the present, and proleptic participation in the eschatological future, come together by the grace of God. Taft observes:

> The hours take their meaning not from the Eucharist, nor from Christian daily life as opposed to an otherworldly eschatological expectation, nor from the natural cycle of morning and evening, nor from personal devotion and edification as distinct from the work of the community. Rather, they take their meaning from that which alone gives meaning to all of these things: the paschal mystery of salvation in Christ Jesus.[10]

The Daily Office is based in the recognition of Philippians 1:21: "to live is Christ." To be conformed to Christ is to die to self and be raised to new life in him (see Col. 2:12-13; Galatians 2:20; Romans 6:3ff.). The Daily Office, then, is not an escape from everyday life but is an intimate expression of the presence of the Risen Christ within that life. In it we seek to do today what the writer of the Gospel of Luke and the Acts of the Apostles did: make explicit the application of the saving and sanctifying grace of God in Christ.

The Daily Office is always a corporate act. The importance of this sense of communal action is especially important since for many of us praying the office often appears to be a solitary act rather than a communal one. According to circumstances, I may pray the office in the physical presence of others, or individually by myself, but either way, I am part of a larger community of my brothers and sisters.

Specifically, that community includes those who are praying the same form of the office, but it also includes others who are praying various forms of that office. Just as praying "Our Father" can never be individualistic, even when prayed privately, so the Daily Office is always communal in nature, even when not prayed "in community."

In this it is essentially different from "private" or "personal devotions". It is always an act of the Church, and we pray it with the Church throughout the ages and around the world. The Daily Office is a communal celebration of who we are and what we are called to be in Christ.

We become a community by what we do in common. Without common action, there is no community. For example: whether or not a group like the Order of Saint Luke is a religious community or just another organization is dependent on what is done together, and that has its most frequent and consistent expression in praying the Daily Office. So Robert Taft writes:

> If what we are as a group is the Body of Christ, and if the eternally present Christ is an everlasting hymn of praise and glory before the throne of [God], it is our vocation to enter into this salvific event, to live that Christ-life of priestly praise and glory.[11]

The Daily Office is rooted in the praise of God which grows out of the proclamation of God's saving deeds. In the words of the *Magnificat*: "The almighty has done great things for me! Holy is [God's] name!" (Luke 1:49) Taft identifies in these words the core of biblical prayer: remembrance, praise, and thanksgiving, and he notes that these give rise to our prayers for God's saving and healing care to continue in the face of our present needs.[12]

The Daily Office is the Church's school of prayer, through which the Church teaches us ways of prayer which transcend time and place and teach us how to glorify God in Christ as a community of God's people. For Taft, the Daily Office is

> a sanctification of life by turning to God . . . to celebrate and manifest in ritual moments what is and must be the constant stance of our every minute of the day: our unceasing priestly offering, in Christ, of self to the praise and glory of [God] in thanks for [God's] saving gift in Christ.[13]

Inner Structure of the Daily Office

The heart of prayer in the Daily Office is found in the psalms, the prayer book of Jesus and the early Church. Praying the psalms is an essential ingredient in the liturgy of the hours. They speak both for us and to us, teaching us how to pray. I believe that the other basic element in the Daily Office can be found in the "evangelical canticles" — those great songs of the early chapters of Luke's gospel which the Church has sung in the Daily Office since ancient times: the Song of Mary or *Magnificat* (Luke 1:39-56), the Song of Zechariah or *Benedictus* (Luke 1:68-79) and the Song of Simeon or *Nunc Dimitis* (Luke 2:29-32). The Church has prayed them day in and day out, year in and year out, and never exhausted their spiritual depth. We begin by praying them; in due season, we find that they pray us into a deeply sacramental spirituality.

Identifying certain times of the day as set apart for prayer has its roots in traditional Jewish practice and the experience of the early Church. Those "hours" which developed as times when the whole congregation gathered to pray are called *"cathedral offices"* or *"people's offices"* to distinguish them from the *"monastic offices"* which monks and nuns were to pray.[14] One might say that when members of an order pray the Daily Office, individually or corporately, it is a "monastic office." When we have morning or evening prayer for our congregation, it is a "people's office." People's offices had to be more open to appropriation by the entire community. There were usually two of these people's offices: morning and evening prayer. To these I would add the Vigil services before the great feasts of the Church (e.g. Christmas and Easter) and preceeding each Lord's Day (the weekly "resurrection vigil" on Saturday evenings. With regard to the cathedral offices, Taft observes:

> Christians by faith had the supreme joy of knowing that they lived a new life in Christ, a life of love shared with all of the same faith. What could have been more normal then, than for those who were able to gather at daybreak to turn the first thoughts of the day to this mystery of their salvation and to praise and glorify God for it? And at the close of day they came together once again to ask forgiveness for the failings of the day and to praise God once more. . . . In this way, the natural rhythm of time was turned into a hymn of praise to God and a proclamation before the world . . . .[15]

In addition to these two offices, monastic practices added a number of others. The number and names of the "hours" varies. We will not undertake to trace those variations, but rather note the way in which the Daily Office can enable the sacramental life. For an overall structure, we will take our cue from Psalm 119:164: "Seven times a day I praise thee." We will identify the inner dynamics and content of a full cycle of seven "hours" for prayer. These are the same offices described by Basil the Great in the fourth century.[16]

There are two "great" offices, common to people's offices, monastic offices, the Anglican *Book of Common Prayer*, the *Lutheran Book of Worship*, Presbyterian *Daily Prayer*, and *The United Methodist Hymnal*: **Morning Prayer** (also known as Lauds) and **Evening Prayer** (traditionally known as Vespers or Evensong).

A third office common to both people's and monastic patterns is the **Vigil**, which our congregations may know primarily from Christmas Eve and the Easter Vigil. **Compline** (bedtime or night prayer), a later addition to the cycle, is widely appropriated because it fits the pietistic as well as the historic practice of praying at the end of the day. To these we add the "diurnal" or daytime hours — the "little hours" they are sometimes called — very brief offices for **mid-morning, mid-day, and mid-afternoon.** These offices may be appropriated in a variety of ways, but their capacity for nourishing the sacramental life, whether of individuals or communities, has been witnessed to by the Church through the ages.

EVENING PRAYER

In the third century, Cyprian wrote:

> At sunset and the passing of the day it is necessary to pray.
> For since Christ is the true sun and the true day, when we
> pray and ask, as the sun and the day of the world recede, that
> the light may come upon us again, we pray for the coming of
> Christ, which provides us with the grace of eternal light.[17]

In keeping with Jewish tradition and that of the early Church, evening prayer always participates in the observance of the following day. (Thus, a Christmas eve service is a celebration of Christmas, not an observance of Advent, and the Easter Vigil is not a Lenten service, but a celebration of the resurrection.) Hence, Saturday evening prayer is a part of the "Lord's Day" observance.

The evening office begins with a Service of Light (from which the lighting of the paschal candle at the Easter Vigil derives[18]) This is an ancient practice, for Tertullian (c. 220) refers to the blessing of the evening lamp.[19] The third century *Apostolic Tradition* describes a very complete service of light, including an opening dialogue and a thanksgiving for the light which begins:

> We give you thanks, Lord, through your Son Jesus Christ
> our Lord, through whom you have shone upon us and re-
> vealed to us the inextinguishable light.[20]

Basil the Great, who died in 379, tells us that the thanksgiving for the light made use of the *Phos hilaron*, which was already ancient when he knew it, making it the earliest non-scriptural hymn we have:[21]

O gracious Light,
  pure brightness of our everlasting God in heaven!
O Jesus Christ, holy and blessed!
Now as we come to the setting of the sun,
  and our eyes behold the vesper light,
we sing your praises, O God:
  most holy and blessed Trinity.
You are worthy at all times
  to be praised with happy voices.
O Son of God, O Giver of Life,
  and to be glorified through all the worlds.[22]

By lighting a flame we are reminded of the vision in Revelation where "the Lamb is the eternal lamp of the Heavenly Jerusalem, the sun that never sets."[23]

The Service of Light is followed by the evening prayer canticle from Psalm 141 and has been used there since our earliest records of the office. Its antiphon sums up the inner dynamic of this office: "My prayers rise like incense; my hands like the evening sacrifice." According to Chrysostom, this psalm was chosen by the early Church for vespers because of its expression of repentance.[24] We will discover that confession is not an essential part of most of the other offices, but it seems to be an important part of the dynamic of evening prayer as Basil the Great points out:

And when the day is finished, thanksgiving should be offered for what has been given us during the day or for what
we have done rightly and confession made for what we have
failed to do — an offense committed, be it voluntary or
involuntary, or perhaps unnoticed, either in word or deed
or in the very heart . . . . For the examination of past actions is a great help against falling into similar faults again.[25]

While the psalms seem always to have been used in the Daily Office,
the way in which other scripture is used varies greatly. Whether there are
several lessons, one lesson, or even none, however, the Gospel is always
proclaimed at Evening Prayer in the words of the Canticle of Mary (The
Magnificat; Luke 1:39-56). Here we find praise, holy memory, care for those
on the margins of life, and God's faithfulness to the covenant people. It is
the language of prayer and praise.

This historic prayer of the Church is brought near at hand in a time of
prayer which may be developed in a variety of ways, including free prayer,
collects, bidding prayers, and litanies, but concluding with the Lord's Prayer,
and acts of going forth.

Evening Prayer seems meant to be sung insofar as possible (hence one
of its names: Evensong). It is built around a service of light, a time of
confession and assurance (traditionally including Psalm 141), the proclamation of scripture (always including the Canticle of Mary), a time of
prayer, and going forth. Within and around this basic structure, many
variations are possible. In connection with a feast day or holy day, we may
speak of "solemn vespers," indicating a full and complete service with singing, several readings from scripture, and the use of relevant visual and
kinesthetic symbols.

In it, we share the request of the disciples on the road to Emmaus:
"Stay with us, Lord, for it is toward evening and the day is almost over"
(Luke 24:29).

COMPLINE

The end of evening activities and preparation for sleep signalled to
monastic communities a need for a "bedtime" office. Indeed, prayers upon
retiring were part of the Judaic heritage. Sleep was understood by the
medieval Church to be a "rehearsal for death" (The children's prayer "Now
I lay me down to sleep" preserves that tradition; its reference to death is
otherwise disconcerting to the modern ear!)

This is a quiet, simple office. It may include a night hymn, a brief confession and assurance, a psalm (Psalm 4 is often used), a *brief* scripture passage and time of silent reflection, a time of prayer including the *Kyrie* (Lord, have mercy), prayer for the night, and commendation.[26]

The historic core of this office is found in the Song of Simeon, the evangelical canticle found in Luke 2:29-32, known to the Western Church as the *Nunc Dimittis*. Before sleep or at the hour of our death, we pray to go in peace, secure in the promise of Christ. We have seen the Savior of all the world, a light to all nations and the glory of God's own people.

In some monastic traditions (and in some settings today), the end of this office is the beginning of the "great silence," with everyone "keeping silence" until Morning Prayer (broken only by the mid-night Vigil, if that is observed). In some communities where I have prayed this office, individuals would remain in prayer and meditation, and then leave quietly when ready.

This is an office capable of great adaptation to place and circumstances. One can pray it at the close of an evening meeting, gather to pray it with a small group, or pray it as a solitary office before going to bed. In any case, we are bound together with the whole Church offering ourselves and our work into God's care and keeping.

VIGIL

What we are calling the Vigil has appeared in many forms under many names. Its earliest form seems to have been a service which lasted the entire night before a great festival or holy day (hence, we speak of "keeping vigil"). It has also been known as a mid-night office,[27] or was divided into a series of "little offices" known as *nocturnes* punctuating the night with prayer for monastic communities (sometimes called "vigils").

Contemporary appropriations are no less precise. It can be a service of preparation for a festival or holy day. As such, it can be prayed at midnight or transferred earlier in the evening, being joined with or even replacing Evening Prayer and Compline. It can function as a mid-night office (perhaps it is used most often this way while on retreat). Or it can serve as the basis for an all night vigil, starting with the service of light at evening prayer and concluding with morning prayer and eucharist at dawn.

Its inner dynamics include two themes: the eschatological expectation (the bridegroom comes at night and we must be waiting, lamps in hand — cf. Matt. 25:1-13); and cosmic praise (those at vigil join with the angels and all creation in praising God while the world sleeps). Thus, in a third century text sometimes (but doubtfully) ascribed to Hippolytus:

Let each one take care to pray with great vigilance in the middle of the night, for our fathers have said that at that hour all creation is assiduous in the service of praising God, all the angelic hosts and the souls of the just bless God. For the Lord testifies to this saying: 'In the middle of the night there was a cry: Behold, the bridegroom has come, go out to meet him.' (Matt. 25:6).[28]

"Cathedral" or "people's" vigils had several forms: a) a weekly "resurrection vigil" on Saturday evenings using the same readings as those on the Lord's day; b) a vigil of extended readings, such as at Easter and other feasts; and c) occasional vigils which could be longer or shorter to suit the occasion. Contemporary appropriation preserves all three types: in ordinary day-to-day or occasional retreat use, the adaptable "accordion" model (so called because it can expand or contract as desired, with few or many readings, with short or long periods of silence after each reading, and with or without music between the readings); before festivals and holy days, a longer vigil of readings related to the day; and on Saturday evenings, a merger of Evening Prayer and Compline with elements of the vigil to form a weekly "resurrection vigil."

Except during Lent, the great canticle for the Vigil office is the Canticle of the Holy Trinity, traditionally known as the *Te Deum Laudamus*. In it we join with creation and the heavenly host in singing the praise of God. Perhaps we can even sense that the "music of the spheres" and the "songs the morning stars began" sing with us!

MORNING PRAYER

It was natural for a resurrection people to take time in the morning to pray. Already in the third century, Cyprian wrote:

One must . . . pray in the morning, that the resurrection of the Lord may be celebrated by morning prayer . . . . the prophet Malachi testifies that he is called the sun, when he says: "But unto you that fear the name of the Lord the sun of justice shall arise and in his wings there is healing." (Mal. 3:20)[29]

Or, in the words of Basil the Great

In the morning [we pray] so that the first movements of

46

the soul and mind may be consecrated to God, and nothing else be taken into consideration before we have been delighted by the thought of God as it is written: 'I remembered God and was delighted' (Ps. 76:3), and so that the body may not engage in work before the saying is fulfilled: 'To you will I pray, O Lord; in the morning I will stand before you and keep watch" (Ps. 5:4-5)[30]

The structure of Morning Prayer is simple. For whatever reasons, there are fewer historic ingredients to be included here. The office begins with the invitation for God to open our lips that our mouths might give praise. A morning hymn and the morning prayer give praise for the new day, for the new creation, and/or for the resurrection. Usually there will be one or more readings from scripture, but again we always have the proclamation of the Gospel in the evangelical canticle; this time, it is the Canticle of Zechariah, traditionally known as the *Benedictus*. Here we pray together for the "dayspring from on high" to break upon us and to guide us throughout the day. Then, as Christ's body, we carry out our priestly responsibility of interceding for the whole world. There is flexibility in this time of prayer (as there is at Evening Prayer), but it concludes with the Collect for the Day and the Lord's Prayer. We are then sent forth to live out our worship in our daily work.

Taft summarizes the depth dynamic of this service:

> In morning praise we renew our commitment to Christ by consecrating the day through thanks and praise. And the hour provides our symbols. The rising sun, one of the ongoing marvels of God's creation, a source of life and food, warmth and light, leads spontaneously to praise and thanks, and to prayer for protection throughout the day. And since we celebrate what we are, and our core reality is that we have been saved by the saving death and resurrection of Jesus, the rising sun calls to mind that true Sun of Justice in whose rising we receive the light of salvation.[31]

THE DIURNAL HOURS (The "Little" Hours)

There remain for our consideration the three brief offices which punctuate the day with prayer. Each is associated with a part of the Biblical story. With regard to Mid-morning Prayer (traditionally known in the West as *Terce*), Basil the Great writes:

47

Again at the third hour we must stand up to pray . . . recalling the gift of the Spirit given to the apostles at the
third hour (Acts 2:15), all should worship together with
one accord . . . And so we apply ourselves to our tasks
again.[32]

The office is very brief: opening sentences, a prayer focusing on the
gift of the Holy Spirit, an optional psalm, a "Little Chapter" (the brief
passage of scripture we encountered in Compline — only a verse or two),
the Lord's Prayer, and a concluding prayer. Its inner dynamic is to keep us
in touch with the presence of the Holy Spirit.

Interestingly Origen (c. 250) knows only four hours for daily prayer:
morning, noon, evening, night. Because of contemporary cultural patterns, it is more likely that a group will be able to gather for mid-day prayer
at noon than mid-morning or mid-afternoon. Thus, it is sometimes en-
larged and becomes a fuller office than the other two. This is the sixth
hour, the time when Christ was nailed to the cross. That, together with a
recognition that the day is quickly passing and there is much yet to do,
forms the inner dynamic of the office. The traditional "Little Chapter"
from Isaiah 40:30-31 reminds us that we must wait on God for the renewal
of our strength.

The ninth hour (in the Western tradition called *none* (rhyming with
"own" rather than "one") is the time of Jesus' death on the cross. There is
a sense of the passing of time, of much left to do, as well as a recollection
of the paschal mystery. The content and structure of the office is the same
as for mid-morning prayer.

The Daily Office helps to punctuate day and night with sacramental
spirituality, recognizing that there is a deeper reality than appears on the
surface, that God is here and we are Christ's body. Taft's poetic insights
ring true to the experience of those who pray the Daily Office:

> When we rise in the morning and come together to sing
> the praises of God at the dawn of a new day, when we cel-
> ebrate the coming of darkness our faith in the true light of
> the world at evensong, when we keep vigil with the angels
> and the heavenly bodies of the firmament while the world
> sleeps, we are doing, in obedience to the command to pray
> always, what men and women have done since the time of
> Jesus. In every time, in every land and from every race: in
> the privacy of the home, in desert or cave, in peasant hut

and hermit cell, in Gothic choir or country chapel, in con-
centration camp or jungle mission station; at every hour
around the clock someone raises his or her voice in the
prayer of the Church, to join with the heavenly and earthly
choirs down through the ages in the glorification of almighty God.[33]

Veni, Sancte Spiritus! Come, Holy Spirit; pray through us for our times
are in Your hand!

Endnotes

1. E. Schillebeeckx, *Christ the Sacrament of the Encounter with God* (Kansas City: Sheed and Ward, 1963), pp. 13-46.
2. Martin Buber, *I and Thou* (New York: Charles Scriber's Sons, 1958), p.
   11.
3. Ruth Duck, "Wash, O God, Our Sons and Daughters" (stanza 3). hymn
   605 in *The United Methodist Hymnal.*
4. Alexander Schmemann, *For the Life of the World* (New York: St.
   Vladimir's Seminary Press, 1973), p. 15.
5. Pierre Teilhard de Chardin, *Hymn of the Universe* (New York: Harper
   and Row, 1965).
6. D. M. Baille, *God Was in Christ* (New York: Charles Scribner's Sons,
   1948).
7. Dom Gregory Dix, *The Shape of the Liturgy* (London: Adam and Charles
   Black, 1945), chapter 11.
8. Robert Taft, *The Liturgy of the Hours in East and West* (Collegeville,
   MN: The Liturgical Press, 1986).
9. Ibid, p. 361.

10. Ibid, p. 334.
11. Ibid, p. 347.
12. Ibid, pp. 357-358.
13. Ibid, p. 360.
14. For a contemporary study, see Paul Bradshaw, *Two Ways of Praying* (Nashville: Abingdon Press,1995).
15. Taft, *ibid*, p. 359.
16. Basil the Great (d. 379) in his *Longer Rules (Patrologia Graeca)* 31, pp. 1012ff.
17. Cyprian, *On the Lord's Prayer* 35-36.
18. Taft, ibid, p. 37.
19. Tertullian, *Apology*, 39.
20. Quoted in Taft, p. 27.
21. Basil wrote: "It seemed fitting to our fathers not to receive the gift of the evening light in silence, but to give thanks immediately upon its appearance. We cannot say who was the father of the words of the thanksgiving for the light." (*On the Holy Spirit* 29 (73) as quoted in Taft, p. 38.
22. Adapted by Timothy J. Crouch from the work of Charles Mortimer Guilbert as it appears in the Ordinary for Evening Prayer in *The Daily Office: A Book of Hours for Daily Prayer* (Order of Saint Luke Publications, 1994), p. 2.
23. Taft, ibid, p. 355.
24. cf. Migne, *Patrologia Graeca*, 55 and 427.
25. Basil the Great, *Longer Rules*, op. cit., 37:4.
26. Note the words of Basil the Great: "Again, at the beginning of the night we ask that our rest may be without offense and free from phantasies." *Longer Rules*, quoted in Taft, p. 86.
27. "Paul and Silas have handed on to us midnight as necessary for prayer, as the story of Acts proves, saying: "And at midnight Paul and Silas praised God" (Acts 16:25), and the psalmist also, saying: "I rose at midnight to praise you for the judgements of your righteousness." (Ps. 118:62) Basil the Great, *Longer Rules*, quoted in in Taft, p. 85.
28. Cf. *Canons of Hippolytus*, Canon 27, as found in *Patrologia orietalis* 31, p.397.
29. Cyprian, *On the Lord's Prayer*, 35-36.
30. Basil the Great *Longer Rules*, in Taft, p. 85.
31. Taft, ibid, p. 353.
32. Basil the Great, *Longer Rules*, quoted in Taft, p. 85.
33. Taft, ibid, pp. 370-371.

Six

Living the Sacramental Life:
BAPTISMAL SPIRITUALITY

At a spirituality retreat some years ago, I was asked to choose a new name for myself to be used during our time together. I chose "Pilgrim." I am a pilgrim on a faith journey, but I have chosen not to be on that journey alone. My path is the path of a community of faith, the Church. We walk together with a diverse throng of persons from the past and in the present.

I enter into a special covenant with persons within that larger community who share some of my basic commitments and values. Together we sculpt the faith perspectives which give meaning to life. Together we seek to discover what it means to "walk the walk and talk the talk."

Our prayer and worship needs to be integrally related with our believing and our acting — a dynamic matrix of *lex orandi, lex credendi, lex agendi*.[1] Seeking to live the sacramental life involves Christians with baptismal spirituality. What is at stake is much deeper than some "liturgically correct" perspective on baptism. Our concern is with the vital core of Christian faith.

Basic Affirmations

There are certain key affirmations which are basic to this kind of holistic understanding of baptism:[2]

1. Baptismal spirituality is grounded in God's grace.

This affirmation is the foundation on which all the rest of our understandings of the baptismal covenant are based. Gayle Felton rightly insists that "we must revitalize our understanding and experience of the grace of God as the ground of our hope of salvation."[3] United Methodists provide a helpful perspective in the affirmation of *The Book of Discipline* that grace "pervades our understanding of Christian faith and life. By grace we mean the undeserved, unmerited, and loving action of God in human existence through the ever-present Holy Spirit." (¶ 66)

John Wesley taught that by grace God is at work within us before we are aware of it. This is as true for adults as it is for infants. For all of us, prevenient grace is

> the divine love that surrounds all humanity and precedes any and all of our conscious impulses. This grace prompts our first wish to please God, our first glimmer of understanding concerning God's will and our 'first slight transient conviction' of having sinned against God. God's grace also awakens in us an earnest longing for deliverance from sin and death and moves us toward repentance and faith.[4]

The baptismal covenant celebrates what the hymn-writer experienced: "I sought the Lord, and afterward I knew . . . it was not I that found, O Savior true; no, I was found of Thee." *(Anon.)*

This amazing grace of God not only seeks us out and prepares the way for us, but also acts in Jesus Christ to save us, and through the Holy Spirit sanctifies us. In the words of the Baptismal Covenant service: "All this is God's work."

Our understanding of the primacy of grace in the baptismal covenant cannot stop there, however. A sacramental spirituality must consider how this grace comes to us. John Wesley points us to what he calls the means of grace. For him, as I see it, the means of grace

> are "outward signs, words, or actions ordained by God" to be the "ordinary channels" through which prevenient, justifying, or sanctifying grace are conveyed to us. They are not the only ways in which God works, but they are the "ordinary" ways — the places where God meets us "by previous appointment," as it were.[5]

Gayle Felton calls for a recovery of an understanding of the centrality of the Church as the community of grace. The Church is itself a means of grace, for it is the means through which God chooses to continue to work in the world.

The baptismal covenant is not a sudden intervention of grace into secular life, but a sign of God's living gracious presence permeating life. A sacramental understanding of "sign" is that it not only points beyond itself, but participates in that toward which it points. For baptismal spirituality, then, the event of baptism both celebrates and participates in the grace of God. This is true not only for the individual who is baptized but for the entire community.

The baptismal covenant continues to be for us a means of grace, in which we both celebrate and are incorporated into the grace of God which prepares the way, and reconciles, nourishes and empowers us. In the words of Henry Lyte's hymn, we are "ransomed, healed, restored, forgiven." In a dynamic and ongoing way, baptism is "Christ's act in the Church."[6] Baptismal spirituality lives within the context of the amazing grace of God.

2. Baptismal spirituality involves the response of faith.

God's grace is central, but the response of faith is also essential. As Gayle Felton insists

> For Wesley, the objective grace of baptism, so real and so significant, must nevertheless be fulfilled in a subjective change in the heart of every individual if the journey of salvation was to continue.

This is not some automatic procedure, a magic rite which appropriates this grace through some prescribed activity. I was challenged to provide a definition of faith for the glossary of *By Water and the Spirit*, and discovered it was more difficult to articulate than I had expected. Within a Wesleyan context, I have proposed that faith is

> trust and confidence in, was well as commitment and loyalty to, that which provides basic life orientation for both mind and heart; thus, for Wesley, not only an assent to the gospel of Christ but a full reliance and trust in him as our salvation, which is the free gift of God and the only condition for receiving God's justifying and sanctifying grace. (see John Wesley's sermons, "Salvation by Faith," and "Justification by Faith.")[7]

Faith, then, is not merely intellectual assent, nor is it restricted to some peculiar religious emotion. It encompasses all of life.

When we talk about the response of faith, about whose response are we talking? It is sometimes assumed that it is the faith of the individual being baptized. Those who support "believers' baptism" point out that if we affirm that the baptismal covenant involves the response of faith, we have to come to terms with an infant's capacity to "have faith." While it is true that an infant may have greater faith in terms of "trust" than those of later years, the object of that faith is in terms of immediate care-givers, rather than what we usually think of as "faith in Christ."

Let us start with the affirmation that the response of faith inherent in the baptismal covenant is, at the most fundamental level, the faith of the whole Church. From Pentecost on, the baptismal covenant is the mark of the response of faith for the early Church. The question is not: "Now just what do you think about Jesus, and how do you intend to respond to him?" It is focused in terms of the response of faith which the Church has given:

> Do you confess Jesus Christ as your Savior, put your whole
> trust in his grace, and promise to serve him as your Lord,
> in union with the Church which Christ has opened to
> people of all ages, nations, and races?[8]

Celebrating the baptismal covenant is an ecclesial action, that is, it is something which the Church does. It is itself a response of faith to the "great commission: "Go and make disciples of all nations, baptizing them . . ." (Matthew 28:19)

It is not only the response of faith by the whole Church which is at work here, however, but the response of faith of a particular congregation at a particular time in a particular place. Nurture and *koinonia* are experienced in the immediate context of a specific community of faith. For those who are able to answer for themselves and for those who cannot, the congregation is asked: "Do you as Christ's body, the Church, reaffirm both your rejection of sin and your commitment to Christ?"

This dynamic of faith helps define who we are and where we belong. If the congregation in which the ritual takes place does not respond to God's grace with faith, they cannot fulfill their part in the covenant. The faith of a specific community is the immediate context for any celebration of the baptismal covenant and the "means of grace" through which the covenant is actualized.

Important as the faith of the whole Church and of a specific congregation are, the faith response of individuals is also integral to the baptismal covenant. Sometimes that faith is a conscious decision which can be located in time and place. Sometimes faith emerges over a period of time through the influence of parents or other significant persons. What the baptismal covenant celebrates is the ongoing process of salvation. Among the options I have noted are these:

> 1. We may be born into the community of faith and nur-
> tured by the Church so that faith develops and is
> strengthened over many years. The baptism of such per-
> sons as infants celebrates this growth in faith by the grace
> of God — a grace at work before, in, and after baptism.

2. For some, the process is begun but then interrupted. Parents and the congregation may not be faithful in keeping their promises. The person baptized may choose to remove themselves from the nurturing community and their growth in faith may lie dormant. What was celebrated in baptism remains a promise of grace still seeking to reclaim the person, but lack of faith hinders receiving that gift.

3. For others, God's grace reaches out and calls them into relationship with Christ and the Church. There may be a particular time when an individual accepts that grace and responds in faith. Because it is a time of turning for them, they may speak of it as their "conversion." As these persons are baptized, the Church celebrates their growth in faith by the grace of God — a grace at work before, in, and after baptism. They enter a community where their faith will be developed or strengthened.[9]

Luther says: "when faith comes, baptism is made complete." I believe we must enlarge our appropriation of that truth to include the faith of the whole Church and the faith of a specific congregation, as well as of the individual.

Faith may come before, or during, or after a celebration of the baptismal covenant; it will most frequently involve all three. The faith of the Church and specifically of parents, friends and/or sponsors always precedes and is present in the act; the faith of an individual may precede it or be experienced within it. In the case of an infant, the baptismal covenant points forward toward that individual response, and for all who are baptized, growth in faith is inherent in living out one's baptism.

John Wesley in the *Treatise on Baptism* puts it this way: "Baptism doth now save us if we live answerable thereto — if we repent, believe, and obey the gospel...." Therein is the challenge of faith, to those baptized as adults as well as to children and youth. Faith is not a momentary act but an ongoing process, and the baptismal covenant celebrates the on-going transformative process by which we seek to live "answerable thereto" by grace through faith.

3. Baptismal spirituality is both evangelical and sacramental.

Such an affirmation may be implied by an insistence on the role of both grace and faith. Sometimes "sacramental" is equated with the importance of "grace" and "evangelical" with the importance of faith. In our emerging understanding of the baptismal covenant, however, we have seen that grace and faith are interacting poles. In God's economy, grace calls forth faith and faith presupposes grace.

I am increasingly uneasy with talking about holding the "evangelical" and "sacramental" in balance, for that seems to imply that they are different things. A Wesleyan perspective understands the sacraments to be evangelical; that is, they celebrate the good news of God's grace and the human response of faith which grace calls forth.

> Without grace, the emphasis on faith can become centered
> on what we do rather than what God does. Without faith,
> grace becomes a kind of magical guarantee which is not
> reflected in a life of spiritual regeneration.[10]

It is also evident that John Wesley was unwilling to separate the evangelical from the sacramental (as evident in his break with the Moravians). The Lord's Supper could itself be a "converting ordinance," and the life of faith entailed using the "means of grace." Nor is it a separation between words and actions, for evangelical witness must be in deed as well as in word, and the sacraments blend the sign/act with the word, as Luther insisted.[11]

The "evangelical" and "sacramental" poles are a dynamic matrix. The evangelical witness is celebrated in, and empowered by, the sacramental life of the Church. The Christian sacraments are, at their very core, evangelical. Those who center attention on the Wesleys' evangelical revival without attention to their insistence on the sacramental means of grace miss the deeper significance of what "evangelical" means. Those who focus on the Wesleys' sacramental teachings without regard to their place in the evangelical "awakening" cannot appropriate the full sense of what the sacraments signify. A renewed understanding of baptism for United Methodists must include both poles as interactive.

The grace of God in baptism dare not be separated from God's grace in Jesus Christ. Rather "baptism is a way of participating in the grace Christ brings."[12] Hoyt Hickman is right to observe

> Among those seeking the renewal of the United Method-
> ist Church, the most crucial division is not between those
> who favor the evangelical at the expense of the sacramen-
> tal and those who favor the sacramental at the expense of
> the evangelical. It is between those who see the sacra-

mental and the evangelical as opposed — whichever side they favor — and those who see them as mutually support-ive.

Baptismal spirituality is grounded in the good news and God's grace and our response in faith. The baptismal covenant not only talks about grace and points to grace, but manifests the presence of grace. Baptism is a "sign-act" which is "grounded in the life, death and resurrection of Jesus Christ."[13] Thus baptismal spirituality reflects the dynamic matrix of an evangelical/sacramental perspective.

4. Baptismal spirituality is centered in the paschal mystery.

It seems strange to me now that so much of my earlier understanding of the baptismal covenant had so little to do with the paschal mystery. I still believe that baptism is a sacrament of belonging, identity, and minis-try.[14] Underlying those perspectives, however, we must recall once again that

> Christian baptism is rooted in the ministry of Jesus of Nazareth, in his death and in his resurrection. It is incor-poration into Christ, who is the crucified and risen Lord; it is entry into the New Covenant between God and God's people.[15]

I'm convinced that we need to appropriate anew an understanding of the paschal mystery, for nothing else summarizes the fullness of what is at stake here.

The early Church called the festival of redemption which recalled both the death and resurrection of Jesus Christ the "Pasch." But the paschal mystery is more than recalling Christ's death and resurrection as a central part of the Christian story. It carries with it the sense of our becoming incorporated into that story, of letting the ministry, death and resurrec-tion of Christ live through us. In Madeleine L'Engle's novel, The Other Side of the Sun, Honoria (an African princess captured and sold as a slave) says:

> We does our dying when we baptized, Miss Olivia. If it ain't done then, ain't never going to be done properly. When you is baptized your angel gives you a shove and you touch eternity . . . Once you brush against eternity, Miss Livvy, then time and death don't make no never mind.[16]

The witness is the more powerful because it is made by one who has experienced abuse and suffering next-door to death itself and yet maintained her dignity and, in a marvelous way, her freedom, for she is far more free than her persecutors.

We have noted that this relationship is symbolized in a powerful way by the paschal candle. We light it first at the "first service of Easter" (traditionally the Easter Vigil). The darkened Church reminds us of the tomb, and the the candle's light penetrates the darkness in celebration of the resurrection. It shines in our services of worship from Easter through Pentecost, the "Great Fifty Days." If this is not the primary experience of the paschal candle, its significance is apt to be misunderstood.

Additionally, we also light the paschal candle at "services of death and resurrection." The use of this terminology at funerals and memorial services combines with the paschal candle to recall the paschal mystery as the foundational perspective Christians have on death and life.

The third use of the paschal candle, we recall, is at all celebrations of the baptismal covenant. It may be reduced to merely a nice decorative touch at such services, unless we remind ourselves that this is not just any candle, this is the "Easter candle" or more adequately, the paschal candle. It reminds us that in baptism we are incorporated into the paschal mystery.

We die to preoccupation with ourselves and are raised to new life in Christ; we are persons of worth in the kin-dom of God. We die to our fear of death and the power of evil, and are raised with hope and assurance that God is with us, come what may. We die to the power of sin and are raised to life in the Spirit who will nourish us on our pilgrimage as Easter people. Baptismal spirituality not only recalls the paschal mystery of Jesus Christ, but seeks to live that mystery in faithful discipleship.

5. Baptismal spirituality is a process empowered by the Holy Spirit.

In *The United Methodist Hymnal*, we find a section on "The Power of the Holy Spirit." The subsections follow the thrust of John Wesley's sermon "The Scripture Way of Salvation:" prevenient grace, justifying grace, sanctifying grace. If our understanding of the baptismal covenant is grounded in God's grace, we should also recognize that receiving this grace is a dynamic process empowered throughout by the Holy Spirit.

We have already noted that the baptismal covenant celebrates the grace of God which prepares the way for our response; it brings us into right relationship with God and others, nourishing and enabling our growth in discipleship. The Holy Spirit is always at work, preparing, luring, sensitizing, inviting, sustaining, convicting, guiding, judging, reconciling, reclaiming, redeeming, empowering . . . the list of human words seems endless!

We are a Pentecost people. The laying on of hands as a part of one's initial baptism, as well as celebrations of the baptismal covenant when professions of faith and reaffirmations take place, is symbolic of our participation in receiving the gift of the Spirit.

The work of the Holy Spirit cannot be located in a moment of time or a point in space. The Holy Spirit empowers our relationship with God. It is the Spirit who "moves across the face of the waters" in both creation (Genesis 1:1) and baptism.

It is the Spirit who makes dry bones live, coming upon the disciples at Pentecost, empowering them for witness and service. It is the Spirit who provides our gifts for ministry. The fruit of the Spirit is that interlocking matrix of love, joy, peace, patience, kindness, goodness, faithfulness, gentleness, and self-control (Galatians 5:22)

All these facets of our understanding of the presence and work of the Holy Spirit are illuminated even more when we recognize their interrelationship with the baptismal covenant. The words which accompany the laying on of hands make that clear:

> The Holy Spirit work within you, that [being born/having been born] by water and the Spirit, you may be a faithful disciple of Jesus Christ.

The physical act of the laying on of hands is indicative of the relationality inherent in the work of the Spirit, for through the Spirit we are incorporated into a *koinonia* which reaches back into the past and forward into the future, as well as with brothers and sisters of the covenant around the world in the present.

Yet I believe that while the Holy Spirit interpenetrates and motivates, we are not manipulated or coerced. We can resist the Spirit or be open to the Spirit. The amazing thing is that the more we resist the Spirit the less freedom we have, and the less we can be the persons we really are.

Someone who knows how to let the wind carry the sailboat is a better sailor with more freedom of movement than one who forces the boat to resist needlessly, or who cannot discern what the wind is doing. Persons in the early Church would have experienced that. The connection between Spirit and wind (Hebrew: *ruach*; Greek: *pneuma*), so evident and recognized by them, is easily lost in translation.

Baptismal spirituality recognizes that the Spirit is at work long before the act of baptism takes place. The Spirit is at work both in the individual and in the community. The Spirit is at work in nature and in history. The Spirit is at work in the Church and in the world. Baptismal spirituality recognizes the presence and work of the Spirit as preceding, motivating, and sustaining our life as disciples of Jesus Christ.

6. Baptismal spirituality is crucial for discipleship.

If we know what it means to live out our baptism, we will know what it means to be disciples of Jesus Christ. Disciples are those who have died and been raised to new life in Jesus Christ, who have been incorporated into Christ's body, who have been sent forth for witness and service. The baptismal covenant celebrates who we are, where we belong, and what we are about.

Baptismal spirituality has implications for both our being and our doing. To separate the two is fatal. With regard to our being, baptismal spirituality makes us aware of who we are. To know that we are "water-washed and Spirit-born"[17] and are "marked with the cross" is to know who we are. We are called to "live into" that identity, to be "transformed by the renewing of our minds" (Romans 12:2) so that we can become who we really are. The discipleship inherent in the baptismal covenant seeks the nourishment which comes from the "means of grace" upon which Wesley insisted. Included are prayer, reading the Scripture, conferring with other Christians, and receiving the Eucharist. The Christian life is a "confirmation class" from which we never graduate, a living out of the Daily Office in which we "pray without ceasing" (I Thessalonians 5:17), a perpetual Eucharistic offering. Through them, our being is nourished and sustained.

In addition to marking our identity so that we know who we are, a baptismal spirituality reminds us of where we belong. Our discipleship is not a solitary undertaking. We are initiated into a community which includes both the Church catholic at all times and places and its local manifestation in a particular time and place. Baptismal spirituality involves my relationship with other members of the koinonia, the way we worship together, nurture one another, and share our pain and our joy. All who are baptized are grafted into the body of Christ. Here I am called to be accountable, not only to God, but also to my brothers and sisters in Christ.

While this dimension of belonging is fundamental, the discipleship inherent in baptismal spirituality is not located only within the community of the faithful. Discipleship involves ministry manifested through both witness and service. Understanding baptism as one's "ordination" to the ministry of the people of God has been a helpful concept for me. I believe that

> whether or not an actual anointing is done, the laying on of hands carries with it this significant theme. It is an anointing to a task, a mission. It gives us a job to do. To live out our baptism is to let the community of faith nurture us so that we may discover "new opportunities for service where individual gifts and graces are discerned, developed, and used".... All baptized Christians are commissioned — anointed to be in ministry. Living our baptism involves living out our calling to the priesthood of all believers. In the Baptismal Covenant we say to our new brothers and sisters in Christ: "Through baptism you are incorporated by the Holy Spirit into God's new creation and made to share in Christ's royal priesthood" (*The United Methodist Hymnal*, p. 37).[18]

Our baptismal spirituality has essential implications for who we are, where we belong, and what we are about. It is a spirituality of identity, of belonging, and of ministry. It reflects the larger context of sacramental spirituality.

The baptismal covenant is more a process than an event. I started out thinking of baptism as a ritual event and trying to understand what that event meant in and of itself. I was unaware that part of my frustration grew out of an assumption that the grace of God somehow invaded our otherwise secular life in the sacraments. This "interventionist" understanding of the sacraments did not square with the theological affirmation which I held: "*vocatus atque non vocatus, Deus est*" (invited or uninvited, God is present). The sacraments are signs of God's living and gracious activity from creation through consummation, permeating Christian life.

There has been a shift in my use of language across recent years. Instead of talking about "baptism," I now choose to talk about the "baptismal covenant." Baptism refers to the ritual act itself; the baptismal covenant implies the understanding which it reflects and calls forth. The baptismal covenant includes (1) the baptism of infants, youth, and adults, (2) the first public "profession of the faith into which we were baptized," (3) subsequent reaffirmations of that faith by individuals, (4) reaffirmations of that faith by the congregation, and (5) the spirituality and implications for discipleship which are part of our understanding of it. In all of these, both the celebration of God's grace and the response of faith to that grace are essential.

The event of baptism is still important. It not only points to that gracious presence of God, but manifests it with special intensity. It is a sacred time in which we can become aware that God's grace surrounds us and interpenetrates our lives. But what it manifests is not God's grace intervening in that moment alone, but in all moments. Baptism is a special grace, a special gift, because it enables us to see and celebrate that actuality.

Because the baptismal covenant is not restricted to the times we celebrate it, we pray for the Holy Spirit to "wash away their sin and clothe them in righteousness *throughout their lives.*" It is not some momentary magical act, but a dynamic and ongoing process which we proclaim and celebrate. Not only do we participate in God's renewing power in the moment of baptism, but the offer of God's forgiving grace throughout life. In baptism, God's grace at work in the present reaches back to the past and forward to the future. A baptismal spirituality, then, must be concerned with this wider and deeper understanding.

What are the implications of this kind of baptismal spirituality for the life of the Church? Let us look at two specific areas as examples.

Inviting to discipleship

Baptismal spirituality, as we have seen, is grounded in receiving and proclaiming the grace of God. Baptismal spirituality that is not concerned for evangelism does not take seriously the good news of God's grace; who could know the wonder of that good news which is intended for all, but keep it to themselves?

Baptismal spirituality may help us understand what the good news is all about. If evangelism is inviting people to discipleship, we need to know the nature of that invitation. The centrality of God's grace must not be obscured by judgment and condemnation. Nor is God's grace coercive. Thus we seek not to manipulate people, but to witness out of our own experience and to invite them to share the good news we have come to know.

Baptismal spirituality knows that this proclamation of the good news is centered in the paschal mystery. Wesley's directive to "show them Christ" is understood to include Christ's ministry and death and resurrection, but also how we are invited to be incorporated into that paschal mystery. It is not an invitation to hero worship, but to take up one's cross and follow, to share in the death and resurrection to which we are called.

Our invitation must also recognize that discipleship is communal in nature. To follow Christ is to become a part of a community of disciples. The invitation is not to Jesus Christ apart from a community of faith, and even less to a congregation apart from Christ, but rather to the Christ who calls us into *koinonia*.

In the process of extending this invitation we must learn to balance hospitality and integrity. If we are arrogant in our possession of the good news and make up a tightly knit but closed group, persons will feel unwelcome and unwanted. If we do not know who we are and what we are called to be and do, our invitation will be empty. The very act of celebrating the baptismal covenant is always a proclamation of the good news. Baptismal spirituality, by its very nature, is evangelical.

Nurturing for discipleship

Nurture is part of our responsibility for both children and adults. Nurture should not be seen as option. Christian nurture is a "means of grace." Many congregations take this the most seriously for children through the age of "confirmation" or youth activities. But unanswered questions may remain: What are we doing for those of ages and stages beyond the pattern our program seems to be addressing? Who is being forgotten? What are their needs? How can we provide an arena in which they can be nurtured in the faith?

What about those who are baptized, whether as children or adults, who then move out of the life experience of the Church? Do we make any effort to keep in contact with them, continuing to care for them, and gently but persistently inviting them to be a part of us?

We need to continue to celebrate the first public profession of faith in the context of the baptismal covenant and there must be a special time of preparation for it. How can we make the experience significant rather than rote? What are the implications of baptismal spirituality for preparing persons for that profession?

There are three parties involved in the baptismal covenant: God, the community, and the individual. What does being faithful to the vows we take as a community mean for us in this congregation at this time in history? Baptismal spirituality includes responsibility for nurture.

Seeking the Sacramental Life

There is no corner of life, whether of the individual, the community of faith, the society, or the world, left untouched by a baptismal spirituality. In all these dimensions, the baptismal covenant celebrates the grace

63

of God which is already at work, the paschal mystery which incorporates us into that work, and the empowering presence of the Holy Spirit. The pieces began to fall into place for me when I recognized that a baptismal spirituality affirms:

> We are a Christmas people, celebrating Emmanuel — God-with-us in Jesus Christ. We are an Easter people, formed by the paschal mystery of Christ's life, death and resurrection. We are a Pentecost people, praying for and being empowered by the Holy Spirit.[19]

Veni, Sancte Spiritus! · Come, Holy Spirit and empower us for sacramental living through a baptismal spirituality!

Endnotes

1. Cf. Keith Irwin's article on "liturgical theology" in *The New Dictionary of Sacramental Worship*, Liturgical Press, 1990).

2. The material which follows grew out of the work contained in *By Water and the Spirit: A United Methodist Understanding of Baptism* (Nashville: Cokesbury, 1993). Reflections on that study were the focus of a retreat sponsored by the Order of Saint Luke resourced by Gayle Felton and Hoyt Hickman. The substance of their presentations and responses, as well as my own reflections are contained in *Doxology*, Vol. 11 (1994). Together with a series of articles on Baptismal Spirituality which appeared in *Sacramental Life*, these writings provide the major part of what appears in this chapter.

3. All quotations from Gayle Felton and Hoyt Hickman containedi n this chapter are taken from the articles in the issue of *Doxology* cited above.

4. ¶ 66, *The Book of Discipline of The United Methodist Church* (Nashville: The United Methodist Publishing House, 1992).

5. *By Water and the Spirit*, p. 33.

6. See Laurence Hull Stookey, *Baptism: Christ's Act in the Church*, (Nashville: Abingdon Press, 1982).

7. *By Water and the Spirit*, p. 33.

8. All references to the Baptismal Covenant service are taken from "Baptismal Covenant I" in *The United Methodist Hymnal* (Nashville: The United Methodist Publishing House, 1989).

9. *By Water and the Spirit*, p. 19.

10. Ibid., p. 11.

11. Cf. Luther's *The Babylonian Captivity of the Church* in Martin Luther, *Three Treatises*, second rev. ed. (Philadelphia: Fortress Press, 1970).

12. *By Water and the Spirit*, p. 12.

13. Ibid., p. 40.

14. See the author's series of articles on baptismal spirituality in *Sacramental Life*, 1992-93).

15. *Baptism, Eucharist and Ministry*, (Geneva: World Council of Churches, Faith and Order Paper No. 111, 1982), p. 2.

16. Madeleine L'Engle, *The Other Side of the Sun*, (New York: Farrar, Straus & Giroux, 1971), p. 210.

17. See "Wash, O God, Our Sons and Daughters" No. 605 in *The United Methodist Hymnal*.

18. *By Water and the Spirit*, p. 29.

19. Ibid., p. 22.

Seven

Living the Sacramental Life:
THE SPIRITUALITY OF THE PASTORAL OFFICES

God is creatively present in all of life, sustaining and enabling persons with grace and love. That presence is recognized in certain events which celebrate and enable us to acknowledge the grace of God at work within and among us. Whether or not we choose to call them sacraments, they are "sacramental" — manifesting the sacredness of life and revealing God's grace and love to us. This revelation comes to us through Christ and is celebrated by the Church.[1]

Seeking to live the sacramental life involves not only a basic perspective on how we view our experience (chapter five), or the distinctively Christian perspective found in a baptismal spirituality (chapter six). It has a pastoral dimension as well — pastoral not in the sense of what ordained clergy do — but in terms of who the Church is called to be.

Jesus Christ is the Good Shepherd, and the ministry of shepherding is entrusted to us. The twenty-third Psalm helps me understand what "shepherding" involves. It may be helpful to think of the service in which persons make a life-covenant together, rites of reconciliation, anointing for healing, "last rites," and the service of death and resurrection as "pastoral offices." Whether traditionally led by clergy or open to lay celebration, they are acts of the Church. Reflecting on the "Shepherd psalm" in relation to these "pastoral offices" has enabled me to see their interconnections and the way in which they can be sources of nourishment for my own spirituality.

Covenanting Together[2]

In a world beset by separation and faithlessness, we dare to invite persons to green pastures as they covenant together in Christ's name. We celebrate the nourishment that comes from life together. We are created for one another. The theology underlying this spirituality is not restricted to the marriage of a man and a woman. Its deeper truth is evident in all covenanted relationships, whether between two partners, or among a group of people (of which a religious order is one example).

In the marriage covenant, for example, two persons "come to give themselves to one another."[3] By so doing, they not only reflect, but participate in, the rule and reign of God. The couple establishes, in the words of Alexander Schmemann, "a kingdom, a little Church, and therefore a sacrament of and a way to the Kingdom."[4] In one sense, they are the prime ministers and priests of this "principality."

There are at least three parties to such covenants. Thus, we invite partners to "enter into union with one another through the grace of Jesus Christ, who has called you into union with himself through baptism."[5] The sovereign of the realm is the Good Shepherd who provides the nourishment and strength of the green pastures supplied by God. As James White observes:

> What God does for us in Christian marriage is a self giving
> of strength and support to human love, reinforced by the
> presence of the community and the community's blessing.
> Christian marriage is a matter of covenant with God that
> a community supports.[6]

The community of faith is thus an important part of this covenant act. As a community, we ask God to confirm the covenant the couple makes and to fill them both with grace.

Covenanting together reminds us that we are meant to live in community. Our families, churches, and covenant relationships are colonies of the realm and rule of God. Sometimes that reality is very dim. Sometimes we betray our trust. Sometimes we are faithless. But God is faithful. In the words of one opening prayer:

> You love us even when we are disobedient.
> You sustain us with your Holy Spirit.
> We rejoice in your life in the midst of our lives.[7]

In such a covenant, we discover the dynamics involved in giving ourselves to another, and what is true of commitment to another human being reveals profound insights into the nature of our commitment to God. The persons involved cannot know where their commitment will lead or what it will entail. Yet that commitment is unconditional: "for better for worse, for richer for poorer, in sickness and in health."[8] Such words recall the covenant prayer: "Let me be full; let me be empty; let me have all things; let me have nothing."[9]

Walter Kasper reminds us that in such covenants

> one touches the ultimate mystery of his or her existence:
> this mystery concerns one deeply and yet remains hidden.
> People commit themselves, in other words, to something that
> they do not possess and that they will never fully possess.[10]

That is also true of our relationship with God. We are always pilgrims on the way. Despite our reservations and failures, we keep being summoned to unconditional commitment. We act to make that commitment real, believing that even our incomplete understanding of what we are about participates in the reign of God. Like covenants between partners, our commitment is "an epiphany of the love and faithfulness of God that was given once and for all time in Jesus Christ and is made present in the Church." [11]

In celebrating these covenants, we affirm that God is at work creating the reign of God among us through colonies of faith and trust which manifest the nature of God's rule. We find a reflection of our own commission in the words of the dismissal:

> Go to serve God and your neighbor in all that you do. Bear
> witness to the love of God in this world so that those to
> whom love is a stranger will find in you generous friends.[12]

It is the love of God which provides the green pastures in which our covenants may be nourished and sustained.

Healing and Wholeness

An honest reading of the gospels forces us to recognize that healing was an important part of the ministry of Jesus. We know from reading the book of Acts that it was a part of the life of the early Church. The directive of the writer of James is clear:

> Is any among you sick? Then call for the elders of the
> Church, and let them pray over you, anointing you with
> oil in the name of the Lord; and the prayer of faith will
> save the sick and the Lord will raise you up; and if you
> have committed sins, they will be forgiven. (James 4:14-
> 15, adapted from the RSV)

Yet the development of the science of medicine and the exploitation of healing by healers whose methods and theology we abhor have conspired to make many leave the field in dismay. If the prayer does not have the desired effects, the conclusion often is that either the sick person or the person praying lacks faith. That engenders additional guilt which may make the situation even worse. If we are to reclaim the pastoral office of healing, we need to adjust our thinking about healing and not allow those who have misused it to determine what is involved.

First, we need to recognize that we may not have forsaken the area of healing as much as we think we have. We do pray that God will work in and through and beyond the medical team. In our private prayers, we may pray with persistent petition for healing. In our counseling and through our caring, we seek to bring wholeness to mental and emotional and social dimensions of life. But often we have not named it, and even less frequently have we put it within a framework of prayer and ritual which would give added significance to what we are already doing.

Second, we have been deterred because of our confusion of the rite of healing with magic. In magic, if the human functionary says the right words and does the right acts, the "powers" are constrained to do what is demanded. If it doesn't work, the magician did something wrong. The "faith-healers" often imply a similar understanding.

Yet we believe that God is sovereign, not some cosmic bell-hop who is constrained to meet our every wish. The truth of the matter is we do not know what wholeness is for any given individual. Sometimes it is the healing of the spirit rather than the healing of the body which is most needed. Sometimes it involves what is called the "healing of memories." And sometimes, I have come to believe, God answers the prayer for wholeness through the gift of death. The prayer of faith involves the trust that God is good and loving. What we do is open ourselves to be channels of God's power, so that the reign of God may be manifested in our midst.

A natural setting for this pastoral office is in connection with the celebration of the Eucharist, for as Browning and Reed put it, "the Eucharist is probably the primary sign to us of the healing of the world and of its intended wholeness in God."[13] To invite those who desire prayers for wholeness to come forward either after the service or within it may call forth a surprising amount of response. .

The importance of the community is affirmed by James White's insistence that

healing is the response of the entire body of Christ to sickness or injury in some part of the body united by baptism.
Thus, it is always a corporate expression of faith in God's
will to health.[14]

The symbolic power of the laying on of hands is great. We manifest it
when we hold the hand of those with whom we pray. Touching the person
puts us in contact with them in a visible way. The touch should be gentle
and reassuring, for we are "touching in God's name."[15] Christ's ministry of
healing grew out of compassion for people in their needs.

As we minister in Christ's name, we become aware that we, too, stand
in need of being made whole. In our need, we want to be able to pray with
the psalmist: "Thou annointest my head with oil; my cup runneth over"
(Psalm 23;5b KJV). We need to be touched by others through whom God
is at work to restore us to wholeness, Part of our own healing involves
reclaiming the pastoral function of a ministry of healing and wholeness.

Forgiveness and Reconciliation

Sometimes history plays strange tricks on us. The medieval Church
became preoccupied with guilt and the need for forgiveness. The sacrament of penance became a central experience in its life. The Reformers
were uncomfortable with the belief that the Church through the priest
was the only channel through which forgiveness could come, so they did
away with the sacrament of penance.

Yet they adopted a very penitential approach to the Lord's Supper,
which became for many the most powerful setting for the confession of sin
and assurance of forgiveness. This obscured the nature of the Lord's Supper as Eucharist or thanksgiving. As we reclaim that sense of joyful
Eucharist in the supper, we must also reclaim the pastoral office of forgiveness and reconciliation. To ignore sin and guilt does not cause it to go
away, but only to fester up in our lives with devastating results. Reconciliation is part of living out our baptism, for "the forgiveness of sins is clearly
identified as one of the forms of self giving that the New Testament Church
experienced in baptism (Acts 2:28)."[16]

Ministering in the name of the Shepherd, we share in preparing a table
of wholeness, acceptance and relationship in the very presence of the en-
emies, sin and guilt. This is a necessary part of healing the whole person
(see James 5:13-16). It is an office in which pastor and people stand bound
together in their need to confess their sin, hear the assurance of pardon,
and be sent forth to do something about it.

Sometimes this will take place within a service of worship, either in response to the proclamation of the Word, or following the opening service of praise. At other times, it may be a special service focused primarily on confession and assurance. Or it may take place within the framework of counseling or visitation. In all settings, the pattern will be similar: a call to confession (often using words of Scripture), a prayer of confession (sometimes followed by the *Kyrie*), and an assurance of pardon (again using words of Scripture).

There is one additional element which we must take seriously, and that is how life and our relationships change as a result. We tend to think of forgiveness as dealing with guilt about the past, and so it does. But it also has implications for life in the future. Otherwise, it is what Bonhoeffer called "cheap grace."[17] Our confession of sin must include "intention of amendment" — changing what brought about the sin in the first place, and engaging in acts of love and service which give evidence of the forgiveness we receive.

We are not talking about acts of "penance" which are unrelated to the confession and reconciliation. We are talking about actually living out the rule and reign of God in our lives in specific ways which are related to our past shortcomings. In this way, we can recover the dynamics which "penance" sought to address.

We must resist the temptation to turn this pastoral office into a detailed self-examination which focuses on the sinful things we have done. What is at issue for us is not so much our various sins, but our relationship with God. In so far as what we do cuts us off from God, we need reconciliation. Forgiveness of sins is not aimed primarily at removing our sense of guilt, though that does happen. *Forgiveness comes for the sake of reconciliation.*

As the image of the prepared table in the twenty-third psalm reminds us, the pastoral office of reconciliation celebrates the loving and merciful nature of God, rather than God's judgment and wrath.[18] We need to hear, as well as to say: "In the name of Jesus Christ, you are forgiven."

Walking Through the Valley: Last Rites

Sometimes we think of last rites as a practice only for Roman Catholics, and that, even for them, it was more important in the past than it is in the present. Yet anyone who sits with a family while life ebbs slowly away from a loved one, or who waits and watches as someone moves toward death fully conscious that it is coming, knows the need for some expression of preparation for death and sending forth from this life.

Often the setting may be an intensive care unit in a hospital, or by a bed in a retirement home. Sometimes death comes too quickly for us to be there. But in those situations where death comes slowly, we have the opportunity to minister in Christ's name in a special way.

A friend of ours, dying of cancer, used to say: "take me through the valley."[19] It was his way of asking for the twenty-third psalm with its affirmation: "Yea, though I walk through the valley of the shadow of death, I will fear no evil, for thou art with me" (Psalm 23:4a KJV).

The pattern of this pastoral office is adaptable to varying circumstances, but it will usually include affirmations from scripture (of which the twenty-third Psalm may be the most frequently requested), prayers which entrust the dying person to God, and a sending forth from this life. At the moment of death, a sense of closure is often needed to mark the movement from waiting for death to come to the combination of grief and relief that it has come. In the crucible of the event, I have found myself placing my hand on the head of the deceased, invoking the presence of the triune God, affirming the help of God through a passage of scripture, giving a brief prayer commending the departed to God (in my father's case, it was the *Nunc dimmitis* from the Order of Compline), and concluding with a benediction. "Go forth in peace," a statement resonating with the words heard at Services of Word and Table, is given a new depth of meaning at such a time (as it was when my wife "sang my father over" using Natalie Sleeth's setting of those words). So also is the blessing:

> Now unto him who is able to keep you from falling, and to present you faultless before the presence of his glory with exceeding joy, to the only God our Savior be glory and majesty, dominion and power, through Jesus Christ our Lord, both now and forever more.
>
> (Jude 24-25)

In the presence of the mystery of death, persons do not quite know what to do. We need to provide a pastoral office which speaks significantly and certainly about the presence of God within the context of that mystery.

In such situations we are reminded of our own impending death. We do not know if we will have time to say goodbye or not, to be sent forth or not. Each time we minister through this pastoral office, we encounter the uncertainty of the time and place of our own death, and the certainty of our own mortality.

Yet in those experiences, we can join in the prayer of the service of death and resurrection:

Help us live as those who are prepared to die. And when our days here are accomplished, enable us to die as those who go forth to live, so that living or dying, our life may be in you, and that nothing in life or in death be able to separate us from your great love in Christ Jesus our Lord.[20]

There are many ways in which the Christian life resembles the worship life of the community of faith. We are called forth and given our identity in baptism, gathered together with other Christians to hear the Word and eat at the Table, and we are sent forth. As a people of hope, we dare to celebrate death not as a "finale" but as a commencement. The pastoral office of "sending forth" a person to the eternal rule and reign of God is not so much a "last rite" as a "rite of passage" through which we hear the apostolic prayer:

May the God of hope fill you with all joy and peace in believing, so that by the power of the Holy Spirit you may abound in hope.   (Romans 15:13)

As we minister in Christ's name, we are taught the inner meaning of what it means to live as those who are prepared to die, and, by God's grace, come to know that we can die as those who go forth to live.

Celebrating Death and Resurrection

Our consideration of the spirituality of the pastoral offices brings us to the service which is frequently referred to as the funeral. Its affirmations are much clearer when we call it a service of death and resurrection.[21] It does not try to minimize the sense of loss we experience. The fact of death is before us in clear and unmistakable terms. But we also celebrate the good news of the resurrection and our covenant relationship with God in Christ.

In this service we find many of the themes we have been discussing. This pastoral office nourishes us by reminding us where we belong, who we are, and what ministry we share. We are reminded that "we are God's children" and that we gather "to praise God and to witness to our faith as we celebrate the life" of the one in whose memory we meet. There is recognition that "we come together in grief acknowledging our human loss."[22] But that is not the final word. The community of faith, of which we are a part, is a people sustained by God's grace, a people who find hope in the midst of sorrow and witness to resurrection in the presence of death. In death, as in life, we are a part of the family of God, and through death we are received by God "into the glorious company of the saints of light."[23]

In this service, as at the Easter vigil and the Lord's table, we participate in the paschal mystery. As Browning and Reed teach us, we celebrate "the *passover* from bondage and death to freedom and life which is God's gift of salvation."[24] The symbolism of dying and rising which we discover in baptism are present once again as we proclaim:

> Dying, Christ destroyed our death.
> Rising, Christ restored our life.
> Christ will come again in glory.[25]

The parallel between putting on Christ in baptism and being clothed with glory in Christ at death is thus affirmed.

The answer to the question of our identity is found in the language of prayer:

> Into your hands, O merciful Savior, we commend your servant _____. Acknowledge, we humbly beseech you, a sheep of your own fold, a lamb of your own flock, a sinner of your own redeeming.[26]

The themes of baptism, Eucharist, and Easter are brought together in ways which mutually interpret one another. Having died in baptism and been raised to new life in Jesus Christ, we are invited to the great heavenly banquet. The words of the twenty-third psalm: "Surely goodness and mercy shall follow me all the days of my life, and I will dwell in the house of the Lord forever" (Psalm 23:6 KJV) are transposed into a new key. It is no longer a reference to earthly time, but to eternity when viewed from the perspective of the resurrection.

This liturgy does not begin when the coffin is carried into the Church. It begins in baptism, is continued at every Eucharist, and celebrated every Easter. As Alexander Schmemann observes, "the whole life of the Church is in a way the sacrament of our death, because all of it is the proclamation of the Lord's death, the confession of His resurrection."[27]

Thus, our ministry is the living out of these themes of death and resurrection. It is the embodiment of the affirmation: "Thanks be to God who gives us the victory through our Lord Jesus Christ" (I Corinthians 15:57).

To seek to live as those who are prepared to die, and to die as those who go forth to live is the nature of our pilgrimage of faith.

When we meet with others on that pilgrimage to celebrate the life of one who has "fought the good fight, finished the race, and kept the faith" (II Timothy 4:7), we are nourished for our own journey. In the presence of death, the priorities of life are reordered. We stand beside our own grave, the grave of baptism, to die once more to self, and to open ourselves to the gracious act of God in raising us to new life in Jesus Christ. As Augustine observed with regard to the Eucharist: "it is your own mystery you receive."

In these pastoral offices, we can discover new insight into living the sacramental life. They remind us of how such moments can become transparent with the Transcendent. *Veni, Sancte Spiritus!* Come, Holy Spirit, and teach us how to live sacramental lives!

Endnotes

1. For a more complete development of this perspective, see Robert L. Browning and Roy A. Reed, *The Sacraments in Religious Education and Liturgy* (Religious Education Press, 1985), pp. 11-15.
2. The illustrations regarding the marriage ritual in this section will be taken from "The Service of Christian Marriage" in *The United Methodist Hymnal*.
3. "A Service of Christian Marriage" in *The United Methodist Hymnal* (op. cit.), pp. 864-869.

4. Alexander Schmemann, *For the Life of the World* (St. Vladimir's Seminary Press, 1973), p. 89.

5. "A Service of Christian Marriage," cited above.

6. James F. White, *Sacraments as God's Self Giving* (Nashville: Abingdon, 1983), p. 88.

7. Ibid., p. 66.

8. Ibid., p. 67.

9. *The Book of Worship for Church and Home*, (The Methodist Publishing House, 1965), p.387. See also *The United Methodist Book of Worship*, p. 291.

10. Walter Kasper, *Theology of Marriage* (New York: Seabury Press, 1980), p. 23.

11. Ibid, p. 30.

12. "A Service of Christian Marriage," cited above.

13. Robert L. Browning and Roy A. Reed, *The Sacraments in Religious Education and Liturgy* (Religious Education Press, 1985), p. 282.

14. James White, *Sacraments as God's Self Giving* (Abingdon, 1983), p. 81.

15. Ibid., p. 80.

16. Ibid., p. 78.

17. Dietrich Bonhoeffer, *The Cost of Discipleship* (New York: Macmillan, 1959), Chapters 1 and 2.

18. See Tad Guzie's chapter on "Comments on the New Form of Confession" in Michael J. Taylor, ed. *The Sacraments* (New York:Alba House, 1982).

19. This was the frequent request of John Stanley Eng, gifted sculptor, whose friendship continues to bless us.

20. "A Service of Death and Resurrection" as cited above.

21. For a commentary on the service see Hoyt L. Hickman, ed. *The Worship Resources of The United Methodist Hymnal* (Nashville: Abingdon, 1989), chapter 9. See also Paul W. Hoon, *A Service of Death and Resurrection* (New York: Abingdon, 1979), and chapter 5 in the *Companion to the Book of Services* (Nashville: Abingdon, 1988).

22. "A Service of Death and Resurrection" as cited above.

23. Ibid.

24. Browning and Reed, op. cit., p. 286.

25. "A Service of Death and Resurrection," as cited above.

26. Ibid.

27. Schmemann, *For the Life of the World*, p. 104.

Eight

Participating in the
Corporate Worship of the Church

They devoted themselves to . . the prayers. (Acts 2:42d)

That worship is important—more important than many of our colleagues in the Church recognize—will get little argument from those who take time to read a book on liturgical spirituality and the sacramental life! Not only do we think worship is important, we want others to join us in living out that affirmation.

But as to the nature of that worship, that may be another matter. We all do our liturgical theologizing out of a given context. What I want us to reflect on in this chapter is the corporate worship *of the Church*, and by that I don't mean that it is something which happens *in* a church building *by* Church people.

I mean that our corporate worship, to have integrity, must be informed by historic liturgical experience.

I do not apologize for being part of those who are called "high Church." I want to work with those who continue to recognize the gifts of historic liturgical practices as resources for worship today. There are other groups whose apostolate it is to keep the experimental perspective alive. I am interested in their work, seek to learn from them, and wish them well.

But I am concerned with the temptation liturgical folk have of letting form become more important than content, of allowing our liturgy to be filled with affectations which look mysterious and feel good and set us apart as seemingly trying to be holier than others. Thus, the question of the nature of the liturgy becomes especially crucial for us.

We must never forget that liturgy (Greek: *leitourgia*) is the public work of the people. After a great festival day in Rome, when everyone from senator and householder to slave became involved in the "clean-up" operation, that was liturgy! As we have noted, it is the people who are "on stage." Worship must be the work of the community, and designers of

77

worship and those who "lead" in its celebrations must never assume that they are the center of the action.

What is it we are about in the liturgy? How can we be constructively critical of our own liturgical practices? And how does that intersect with our concern to discover a Lukan approach to liturgical spirituality and the sacramental life?

We have noted that human beings are, first and most basic of all, "*homo adorans.*" We receive the world *from* God, and offer it *to* God, and by filling the world with this "eucharist" — this thanksgiving, we transform the lives which we receive from the world into life in God.[1] Both Eucharist and the Baptismal Covenant are basic to our understanding of the liturgy of the Church which is embodied in Services of Word and Table and celebrates the living out of the Baptismal Covenant.

A survey of the current landscape in liturgical theology provides some important points of reference. Kevin Irwin reminds us that "Christian prayer and worship are meant to lead us to experience God; they are not substitutes for meeting the living God."[2] Mediating the experience of God is an awesome task, but it certainly gets us away from concern about the peripheral and focuses on the heart of vital worship. It is important for us to be self-critical about our work. Mary Collins insists:

> The contemporary task of liturgical theology is preeminently critical: Is the faith vision being celebrated in the liturgy adequate? Is it congruent with human and ecclesial experience and expectations of the saving grace of Christ?[3]

Further, it is not enough to examine individual parts of the liturgy. We must have a strong sense of its unity. So I. H. Dalmais advises us that

> One must be attentive to the total liturgical action. Thus, each element — text or rite — needs to be interpreted in relation to the other parts of the liturgy. . . . one ought to respect the relationship between individual rites and words and the essentially symbolic character of the liturgy as a whole.[4]

Our challenge in promoting the corporate worship of the Church is found in that penetrating question by David Power:

> Does the word of the liturgy resound as a word within our hearts, so that we are caught up in its movement and not only subjected to the ritual's authority?[5]

78

One further reminder: many attempts to revitalize worship focus either on the "audience" (seeking to be aware of the needs and preferences of the "consumer") or focus on "God" in ways which assume that certain forms and rituals are "revealed theology!" Both, it seems to me are bound to be inadequate approaches to the task. The dialogical nature of liturgy is made clear by Don Saliers:

> Worship is corporate dialogue and communion with God. It is a corporate enactment by word, silence, rite, and song of the community's memories of God so as to invite the presence and power of God to come to awareness. . . . Worship is God centered yet thoroughly grounded in human life; it is theocentric and anthropological at the same time.[6]

With these clues about the essential nature of liturgy as the corporate worship of the Church for a foundation, let us turn our attention to the interconnection between liturgy and spirituality. We have been examining this concern from a variety of perspectives. But let us focus on the liturgy of the Church from the standpoint of those who prepare to celebrate together — those who design and plan worship, and those who prepare to participate in it.

We are burdened by demands placed on us by ourselves and others. The list of things to do seems to grow faster than our ability to get things done. As a result, we are often harried and preoccupied. Prioritizing the tasks before us is essential if we are not to fritter away our energy on immediate demands while the essential mission to which we are committed goes begging. Sorting out what God calls us to do, as over against our self-expectations or those placed on us by others, is a continual process. Unless we are in relationship with the source of spiritual strength, our lives become fragmented and our energies dissipated.

Our problem is not so much finding time as disciplining ourselves to take time, to see the nourishment of our souls to be as essential as the nourishment of our bodies. Without continually returning to the wellspring of our faith, the channels through which empowerment of the Spirit might flow become clogged.

One of the disciplines which help us keep those channels open is the use of the Daily Office. Another is the taking of intentional times (such as one day a month, and/or one week a year) for spiritual retreat. Such experiences are vitally important to our ministry. But they must not be seen as unrelated to what we do the rest of the time, as if spirituality existed in some water-tight compartment set apart from ordinary daily life. Rather, our "times apart" can sensitize us to sources for nourishment which are available in and through our daily work. Preparation for worship can be transformed if we understand it as a resource for our own spiritual growth, as well as enabling the people of God to worship in spirit and in truth.

We can discover a resonance between the life of the community and our own spiritual journey in the festivals and seasons of the Church year. Our sense of identity is developed as we are shaped by the Word, and we can come to a deeper understanding of ministry through the music we use in worship.

Discovering Liturgical Spirituality Through Festivals and Seasons

We do not begin our preparation for worship in a vacuum. The immediate context for our work is provided by the festival or season of the Church year.[7] Advent is not Christmas, nor is Lent Easter. This is so natural to us that we do not stop to think about what it has to say to our spiritual journey. Adolf Adam points to the depth dynamic of this way of keeping time when we writes:

> The paschal mystery, then, is the heart and center of the entire liturgy and thus of the Church year, which is shaped by the celebration of the mysteries of redemption. The paschal mystery is the wellspring whose waters flow through the liturgical year; it is the point on which the entire year turns.[8]

John and Elizabeth Box Price have taught me that if we are intentional about the inner dynamics of these festivals and seasons, we will discover that they provide a way for us to understand the dynamics of our own journey.[9] We may be living in Lent while the Church is celebrating Christmas, but the signs and symbols of both seasons can become instruments upon which we play our own peculiar melody of life, only to discover that it reflects a wider symphony of which we are a part.

The Church year is not linear, but circular. It begins where it ends and ends where it begins. We are used to thinking of the first Sunday in Advent as the beginning of that year and in one sense, it is. Advent is the season of joyful expectation, but that expectation exists in three dimensions. One of those dimensions is focused on the preparation for the celebration of the birth of Jesus Christ. It is a time when we recall the longing for the coming of the Messiah. The great prayer of Advent is to be found in the "O Antiphons" which call out the invitation: "Come!"[10]

However, Advent not only rehearses the coming Messiah in the past, but addresses us in the here and now. Christ comes to us. We long for that coming; we prepare for it; and yet we know that we may miss it. We may be tending to the honored guests of culture rather than seeking the baby in the manger. The third focus of Advent points to the eschatological nature of our faith. We live in anticipation of the consummation. For the ancient Church, this was a time to focus on the coming kingdom. Thus, Advent both completes the year and begins a new one.

The attempt to make Advent parallel Lent was doomed to failure. It has a different mood and temperament. It refuses to act like a somber penitential season, and for good reason. Christ came, Christ comes, Christ will come. That constant theme is our joyful expectation of the coming of Christ. That resonates with our personal journeys. For we, too, "long for life to be different."[11] We wait in joyful expectation to recall Christ's coming in the manger of Bethlehem, to celebrate his coming into our own hearts and lives, and to live in hope for the final consummation. Whenever longing or expectation permeates our lives, we live out the inner dynamics of Advent.

The celebration of the nativity at the Festival of Christmas is surrounded by cultural patterns which threaten to obscure it. One way of responding to that incursion is to reject the whole celebration. To do so would deny that within the manger of popular culture lie significant values which deserve to be separated from the straw.

Our culture tends to confuse Christmas with Advent, and then, once December 25th has arrived, to pack everything away rather quickly and go back to ordinary experience. In the life of the Church, however, we can affirm the nature of Advent in its own right by letting the sense of joyous expectation build, carefully selecting stanzas of familiar carols which have Advent themes, singing Advent hymns, gradually increasing the use of the symbols and music of joyous celebration until Christmas eve.[12] Then the blues and purples of Advent can give way to the celebrative white and gold of Christmas; Mary and Joseph and the baby in the manger can be placed in the creche; and the joyous carols can be sung.

For the Eastern Church, the festival of Epiphany on January sixth was the great celebration, including the story of the coming of the magi, but celebrating the "showing forth" or manifestation (the *theophany*) of God. For the West, the central story became that of the shepherds, and the celebration of Christmas was on December 25. We are heirs to both traditions. Christmas starts with the festival of the nativity on December 25, and ends with the festival of the Epiphany on January 6. Those two festivals begin and conclude the twelve days of Christmas. If we "hold back" on our use of Christmas symbols and music until Christmas eve, we will have a rich treasury available for our use during that season. We can resist "taking down" the symbols of Christmas until after Epiphany, when Christmas is really over.

The gift which we have on our hands is that, with the exception of that peculiar song about the partridge in a pear tree, our culture doesn't know very much about the twelve days of Christmas. The Church is free to reclaim that heritage. There is deep meaning in the way the Western church came to celebrate the first four days of Christmas. The first day of Christmas is the festival of the Nativity; we celebrate the coming of the Word-made-flesh. But the second day of Christmas is the day of St. Stephen the Martyr. It is as though in the midst of all the joyous celebration (which in the culture tends to be quite superficial) we must be reminded of the cost of discipleship. If we receive this newborn babe, we must not forget the cross! The third day of Christmas is the feast of St. John the Evangelist. We are reminded that even though the cost of discipleship is high, the Light that shines in the darkness cannot be extinguished. And then on the fourth day of Christmas, we are plunged into the agony of the murder of the holy innocents, recalling the story of Herod's soldiers killing the babies of Jerusalem. And here we are face to face with all injustice and oppression in our world. It is a day of great lament in the face of the powers of evil around us. Such is the deep meaning of Christmas — a far cry from the cultural festival, indeed.

Our focus during the Christmas season is the gift of God in the Incarnation, and the "Epiphany" or showing forth of that gift to all humankind. Whenever we celebrate the gift of God in our own lives, we live out the meaning of Christmas. Whenever we become aware of the love of God being shown forth to us in special ways, we celebrate Epiphany. Such recognitions focus on the initiative of God. Another dimension to the inner dynamics of this season can be found in our response. When we are able to see the holy in the common things of life,[13] we join in the experience of the shepherds. And when we bring gifts, we share in the mission of the magi. It is much easier for many of us to identify our weaknesses than to recognize that we do have gifts and talents we can present to the incarnate Christ. One of the deep mysteries of our faith is that the gifts we offer are gifts we have received. Seeing the holy in the common, and offering our gifts back to God enable us to live out the inner meaning of Christmas.

The nature of Lent as a penitential season is deeply ingrained in us. It is a time for walking the way of the cross and counting the cost of discipleship. When we wrestle with difficult decisions, and "strategize" the expenditure of our lives, we are living in Lent.[14] Yet we need to recall that the Church does not count Sundays as part of the forty days of Lent. Each Lord's day recalls the resurrection and thus, even in Lent, Sunday is a festival day. We anticipate the glorious victory of Easter, as well as the sacrifice of Good Friday. The symbolic event which ties these themes of death and resurrection together most powerfully is baptism. It is helpful for us to return to the practice of the early Church and find in Lent a time of preparation for baptism and the renewal of baptismal vows.

In reflecting on the significance of our baptism for our pilgrimage of faith, we must face the inner dynamics of both death and resurrection in our own lives. Whenever we do that, we are living in the context of Lent.

The Sunday before Easter combines the themes of exaltation and suffering in yet another way. Two Sundays before Easter used to be Passion Sunday. We stood in the presence of the cross, then backed up the following Sunday to recall the triumphal entry. The common calendar we now use is much more satisfactory, for it allows us to tell the story in a dynamic way on Palm/Passion Sunday. The service centers on that story. It can be told through scripture, music, and drama. Our recollection starts with the triumphal entry (for which the processional becomes a natural re-enactment). But before the service is ended, we are standing at the foot of the cross. This is particularly important for those who attend only Sunday services. Persons who try to jump from the emotional high of Palm Sunday to the celebration of Easter without confronting the cross are thus directed to the crucifixion story in unmistakable terms.[15]

If one temptation in our spiritual pilgrimage is to forget the resurrection by focusing all our attention on the cross, the other temptation is to forget the suffering of the cross by focusing on the triumphant Christ. Both must continually point us to the other, and our growth in grace will reflect the appropriation of the paschal mystery as a whole.

I grew up in congregations which gave a good deal of attention to "Holy Week" — the octave from Palm Sunday to Easter. But even then, there was a sense that something was different beginning with Maundy Thursday evening. For the ancient Church that block of time — from Holy Thursday evening through Good Friday and Holy Saturday and Easter Day —,were the high holy days for Christians, and it encompassed the paschal mystery of suffering, death and resurrection as a whole. As we have already seen, it was sometimes called the "Pasch." Later it was known as the "Triduum"— the three holy days.

One of the most exciting opportunities to hold the entire paschal mystery together comes through our recovery of the Easter Vigil. The service starts in the darkness of the tomb. Then the new light is kindled, the paschal candle is lit, and the *Exultet,* that great resurrection hymn is sung. Vigil readings tell the story of salvation, and we renew our baptismal vows together before celebrating a resurrection Eucharist around the table of our risen Lord.[16]

We can understand why this service was a focal point of the Christian year for the early Church. Once we have experienced its deep significance, we find resonances with our own pilgrimages in which we move from tomb to resurrection by the power of God. We, too, know what it means to be "raised up." It is possible for us to dance on the gravestones[17] and celebrate our new life in Jesus Christ.

The period which follows is the Great Fifty Days — literally *Pentecost* (which is why we no longer refer to the season *after* Pentecost Sunday as Pentecost season!). This time from Easter to Pentecost was a time of great joy and celebration for the Church. Unfortunately, it was overshadowed by Lent in the penetentially- inclined medieval Church, and that baggage was carried over into the Reformation Churches. Lent *is* an important part of the Church year for liturgical spirituality, but just as Christmas should not be overshadowed by Advent, neither should the Great Fifty Days be pre-empted by Lent. The focus gradually shifts from celebration of the presence of the Risen Lord to the promise of the Holy Spirit, and reflection on the importance of the Spirit for the Church and the pilgrimage of faith.

The Great Fifty Days culminate in the third great festival of the Church year, ranking in importance with Christmas and Easter — Pentecost. On the one hand, it is the festival of the Holy Spirit. On the other, it is the festival of the birth of the Church. These two themes are inextricably linked not only by the festival, but also by the third article of the Apostles' Creed. The coming of the Spirit establishes the Church. Receiving the Spirit is therefore not a privatized, individualistic experience. Rather the Spirit is the divine relational power binding us to one another and to God. The Spirit is the renewing force at work in all creation for which we pray in the antiphon to the psalm for Pentecost: "Send forth your Spirit, and renew the face of the earth."[18]

When we pray for the coming of the Spirit, we open ourselves to receiving new power which may lead us in surprising directions. Whenever our longing for the Spirit's renewing strength is poured out in prayer, we prepare for Pentecost to happen in our lives. And when the Spirit descends to empower us, creating bonds of relationship with others who also receive that gift of God's grace, we celebrate Pentecost as a part of our pilgrimage — a moveable and repeatable festival.

What of the other thirty-plus weeks of the Church year, sometimes referred to as Sundays *after* Epiphany, and Sundays *after* Pentecost or Trinity? These are the Sundays of "ordinary time" — and how accurately that mirrors our experience, for ordinary time is where we live out most of our lives. Sometimes we have to put one foot in front of the other and keep on keeping on. The practical labor of putting mortar between the bricks,[19] of building ever so slowly, of sowing seeds even where we will not see the harvest[20], is part and parcel of our pilgrimage of faith. Yet even in ordinary time, time is defined by the living Lord. Each Lord's day is an Easter event, testifying to the resurrection, and sanctifying the ordinary in extraordinary ways.

The Lord's day is ever the center of the Christian year, and in it we come to know we are an Easter people.

But ordinary time is not devoid of festivals. The Sundays after Epiphany begin with the Baptism of our Lord, and conclude with the Festival of the Transfiguration. The Sundays after Pentecost begin with Trinity Sunday, conclude with the Festival of Christ the King, and include the Festival of All Saints. Some of us even persist in continuing to celebrate the Festival of the Reformation, believing that the Church must always be reformed and reforming. These festivals, all too frequently forgotten, remind us that within the ordinary times of life, God is still at work sustaining, reclaiming, and sanctifying us in ways of which we may be only dimly aware.

When we become attuned to the resonance between the Church year and our own journeys, we discover that we are not alone, after all. We are part of a community of faith, the members of which have walked roads amazingly like our own. In an unforgettable image, Ira Progoff has taught us that when you go deep down into the well of your own spirit, you discover that the source of the water you seek is a part of a great underground river connected to the wells of others. The Church year provides us with a map to the channels of grace from which we are nourished.

Another source of nurture can be found in the sanctoral cycle — a calendar of commemorations which provide models of faith for us.[21] Clifton Guthrie, who has developed and edited a contemporary approach to the sanctoral cycle writes:

> It is hoped that those who do appear on the calendar are persons who have lived lives that are 'prayable.' That is, because they are transparent to the character and intentions of God, their lives prompt us both to render thanks

to God and to pray that our lives might become likewise transparent. They are also exemplary, by which is meant both that they are exemplary of the best of Christian witness and that they are examples of people who have lived faithfully within particular social locations.[22]

Developing Identity Through the Word

The community context of our preparation for worship is the Church year, but the focus of that preparation is found in Scripture. Once we have taken into account where we are standing in the life-experience of the Church, we turn to the Bible.

Worship is grounded in the Word of God. It is not primarily a search for God, but a proclamation of God's coming to us.[23] The Bible reflects the experience of persons who were addressed by God, and through their stories and teachings God speaks to us.

That still leaves open the question of what passage of Scripture it is which addresses me. I used to start with a theme or idea or illustration, and then go to Scripture to find something I could use as a text. That approach had some built-in problems.

First, I was restricted to passages which I knew well or which I could locate through a concordance or topical Bible. Second, I brought the agenda to the Word, rather than letting the Word form me. And third, there was no comprehensive approach to the Bible over a period of time.

As has been true for many others, I found the answer to these problems in the lectionary, A lectionary is a table of readings designated to be read over a period of time. An adequate lectionary will reflect the Church year and provide us with a pattern of coming to terms with the depth and breadth of Scripture. It is possible to develop a lectionary on your own. I tried that once for my personal devotional reading. It was a gigantic undertaking, and was not very satisfactory. Later, I learned I didn't have to reinvent the wheel!

Instead, I have come to rely on the three year cycle of the Revised Common Lectionary prepared by the North American Committee on Calendar and Lectionary. One might turn to the use of such a lectionary for a number of reasons: There are many excellent resources available which are keyed to it. It enables those involved in planning worship to coordinate efforts far in advance. It relates us with Christians of other denominations.

But by far the most important factor in spiritual growth comes from the symbolic reminder that God takes the initiative in addressing us individually and corporately. It is not so much that the Word of God gives us answers to our questions, as that the Word helps us know what questions it is important to ask! Furthermore, it is the Church which provides the context in which we read the Word of God. Even when I read the Bible in private, I need to remember that it was written out of the life experience of other persons in earlier faith communities, and that it was addressed to persons within communities of faith. It is the Church which teaches me how to read the Scriptures.

The Revised Common Lectionary enables us to grasp the depth and breadth of Scripture while recognizing the context of the Church year. Being aware of the overall pattern makes that clear. We are not invited to a "tasting party" with little nibbles of Scripture served to us, but to a complete and nutritious meal with four courses. The order in which these lections may be read in worship may not be the best way to read them in preparation.

I have found that it is most helpful to turn first of all to the Gospel lection. From Advent through Epiphany, and from Lent through Pentecost, it controls the choice of the other lections. Each year, one of the synoptic gospels is read in its own right: Matthew in year A, Mark in year B, and Luke in year C. The Gospel of John is read in the festival seasons, and in the Markan year. By living repeatedly with one gospel after another, we are able to discern its themes and implications for our lives. The good news of Jesus Christ is the controlling proclamation for the Church. Those of us who stand when we read it do so, not because it is more truly Scripture than the other lessons, but because it reminds us that it is in and through Jesus Christ that we understand ourselves as we respond to all Scripture.

With the gospel in mind, we can turn to the first lesson. From Advent to Epiphany and from Lent to Easter, it will be an Old Testament lesson related to the Gospel reading. From Easter to Pentecost, it will be a lesson from the book of Acts (with Old Testament alternatives also available). On the Sundays after Pentecost, it will be a semi-continuous reading from the Old Testament. Since Matthew views Jesus as the new lawgiver, during year A we read the patriarchal and Mosaic narratives. Mark affirms Jesus to be the Son of David; therefore during year B we read lessons which reflect Davidic themes. For Luke, Jesus is prophet, so in year C the lessons concern Elijah, Elisha and the minor prophets.

The reading from the Psalter is understood as a congregational response to the first lesson. Being able to pray the psalms because we live with them has been recognized as a vital source of Christian spirituality for much of the Church's life. Unfortunately, for much of recent history the psalms were largely forgotten — except for the "great favorites." The recovery of the regular use of the psalms puts us in touch with the experience of Jesus and the early Church, and opens the channels for spiritual nourishment to come to us in continually enriching ways.

Since Psalms provided the "hymnbook" of the Jewish faith, we do well to recover the practice of singing them, or at least of singing an antiphon for them. As the music of the psalms gets inside us, we find the words coming to mind as a way of expressing our feelings and our faith.

Finally, we turn to the Epistle lesson which is related to the gospel in Advent through Epiphany and Lent through Pentecost, and is read with some degree of continuity during ordinary time.

The temptation is to treat the Bible merely as a sourcebook for worship. As we read it, we can be preoccupied with its use in preaching and liturgy. In so doing, we may insulate ourselves from the nourishment God would give us. Instead, we need to allow ourselves to be addressed personally, so that we can be "shaped by the word."[24] By recalling and reflecting on the Story in light of our hopes and frustrations, our joys and sorrows, our successes and failures, we discover our own identity being addressed, formed, and developed.[25]

Therefore, we need to read in the spirit of prayer. A prayer for illumination is not only appropriate in worship before the Word is read, it is a way of opening ourselves to hear God's word to us as we prepare. We also need to remember what we read for the last Sunday, so that the sweep of the story may be disclosed to us.

Because the lectionary is our servant, we may discover verses before or after the assigned lection which are not prescribed but which speak powerfully to us. We may even find ourselves adapting the lection we read to include such verses, a practice which is most appropriate for those of us for whom the use of the lectionary is recommended but not required.

When we use all three lections and the psalm regularly we find we have received another gift: we have the opportunity to be immersed in Scripture because we plan to use it. We cannot escape from the Word which addresses us.

As we open ourselves to be shaped by it, sometimes because it affirms and strengthens us in our faith, and we say "Amen! Amen!! It really is that way!!!" But there are other times when it calls us to account, making us uncomfortable, and we respond: "Lord, is it I?" only to hear the prophetic word, "Yes, you are the one!"

Spirituality is not a matter of formation only, but of re-formation. That is why John Wesley thought it important to ask: "Are you going on to perfection?" When we stop being changed by the power of God mediated to us through Scripture, our pilgrimage becomes hesitant and erratic. The Word of God addresses us in the here and now within the context of the community of faith. In the Word, we discover who we are, where we belong, and what we are about.

Being Shaped By (the) Service

We have seen how the context of our preparation for worship is the Church year and why the focus of that preparation is found in Scripture. But what of the shape of the service itself? What is the shape of its depth dynamic, a shape that shapes us? If the Service shapes our service, what is the meaning of the word "service" as we use it in both ways?

We discover that it comes from the Latin *servire*, meaning to serve, to be a servant. As a noun, based on the Latin *servitum*, its meaning includes labor done for another, a duty, spiritual serving of the deity, religious duty performed through appropriate rites (thus, any particular celebration of public worship), and conduct contributing to the welfare of another.[26]

In a service of worship, we discover a rich matrix of meaning. In it, we serve God, and that service is both "duty and delight."[27] On the other hand, through our worship, the presence of God's grace certainly contributes to our welfare. While it seems strange to talk of it this way, there is a very real sense in which the service of worship is both our service to God and God's service to us.[28] Nor is that all. For our worship is done to the glory of God both for the life of the Church and for the sake of the world.[29] As the Church, we discover in our worship not only who we are but what we are called to do—to live to the glory of God in a life of service for others.

We can find many manifestations of the worship service itself. But its depth dynamic from the early Church until the present time is amazingly consistent: people gather together, they hear and respond to the Word, they give thanks and share a holy meal, they are sent forth to be Christ's body in their everyday lives. We have already considered the crucial role of the Word and the place of eucharist—the holy meal. But gathering and being sent forth are not merely preliminary preface and concluding postscript, but essential to the inner depth dynamic of worship itself.

In one sense, the service of worship begins when the first person leaves home to "go to worship." It is not "business as usual" but rather "time out" from the ordinary routine to enter into a holy space and time. Trying to blur this distinction in an attempt to make this holy time an experience of the usual (with only usual language, usual symbols, usual actions) ignores the amazing dynamic of this time of communal meeting with God. It is true that God is always with us, but it is not true that we are always aware of God's presence, consciously giving praise to God, seeking to hear God's word to us, sharing at Christ's table, and responding to the ministry and mission given us.

Leaving the worship service to go through the "servants' entrance" into the world is not something that ought to just happen, as if we were saying: "there, that's over; let's get on with doing what we were going to do." No, for if our worship has been vital and honest, we are not the same as when we set out to come to "the service." We may say "we were moved," that is, we are not at the same place we were. And furthermore, we leave as those who are "apostles"—sent out ones, in ministry and mission in Christ's name.

Within this four-fold shape of the service (gathering, hearing, sharing, being sent forth) are other essential ingredients as well: praise, confession and assurance, intercession, and commitment among them. Shot through them all is the sense of being in community—*koinonia*—with our brothers and sisters as we worship. Each of these needs careful consideration as we plan our worship.

Despite what some are telling us, we do not have to re-invent worship. It has served generations of persons in many different times and places with a great variety of life settings and situations. That does not mean that we are bound to the "old time religion" of our grandparents' day, for it, too, may have strayed from the depth dynamic, or kept it in superficial or outworn ways.

We are wise to use the service outlined by our denomination as the basis for our planning. That outline will reflect both historical patterns and contemporary reflection. It is the result of careful painstaking work on the part of many people who can cross-check each other's blind-spots, and seek to avoid fads of the moment. No one of us is wise enough to invent the service of the worship of God. It is not my worship alone, but the community's worship, and not this community's worship only, but that of the Church through the ages and in all times and places.

However, it is possible for us to appropriate this basic pattern only superfi-cially and to miss important cues within it. A retired pastor friend recently asked me: "whatever happened to confession in our services? The Method-ist services I attend don't seem to include it any more." Because it is no longer a major heading (as it was when the outline was the Isaiah 6 model of praise, confession and assurance, word, and response), and because there is direction that it can come either early in the service or as a response to the word, it has become easy to overlook it.

Thus, we must attend first of all to the basic pattern of the worship service. We might call both the "headings" of the service and those parts within them that do not change from service to service the "ordinary" of the service. In a computer age, we can think of the ordinary as the "boilerplate" into which the items that change from week to week can be inserted. Those parts which change (such as scriptures, hymns, prayers) are the "propers." Some may be "propers of the season" (what we use throughout Advent, for example); others will be "propers of the day." When we have taken great care in appropriating the ordinary from our tradition's order, and when we are aware of this service's place in the Church year and the Scriptural basis of the service, specific choices as to propers will be both easier and more difficult. They will be easier because we know what function they are to serve. A call to worship does not call for the same content as a benediction and dismissal, to take an obvious ex-ample. They will be harder because we cannot just pick what we like. Each element must fulfill its function in the pattern and be in relation with the rest of the service.

There is yet one more crucial part of the shaping of the service. For while we are a part of the Church through the ages and around the world, the mystery of the incarnation teaches us that the particular embodiment at this time and place will be unique and yet have connection with all the worship that has gone before and continues around the world. The radical particularity of Jesus' ministry will not let us escape into a "one size fits all" approach to worship. The planner must take the ordinary that re-flects the wider Church and the Scriptural propers in the context of the season and find other propers that speak to this time and place without ignoring the history of the Church nor its world-wide embodiment.

How then does this shaping of the Service help us shape the ser-vice to which we are called? A liturgical spirituality for the sacramental life recognizes that we are called out, set apart for worship and praise and prayer as a community of faith. It will not shy away from the recognition that we are a "peculiar people" as Elizabethan language put it—not differ-ent for the sake of being different, but willing to be different in order to be faithful. Liturgical spirituality is grounded in the hearing of God's word and our response to it. Sometimes this will comfort us as we experience God's healing grace; often it will make us uncomfortable as we face the demands of the gospel. We will embody a eucharistic spirituality—giving thanks to God, offering up what we have been given as well as what we have done with it to God, and receiving it back from God again, blessed for our nourishment and strength. A liturgical spirituality will seek to live out the baptismal covenant that sends us forth in service to the world because of our worship, rather than escaping from the world into our worship.

If we are shaped by the service of worship, we will be shaped to live out the life of the Church in service for the sake of the world. That is the nature of our apostolate, our ministry, our service.

Understanding Ministry Through Music

Recently my wife asked a group of laity to recall what they believed about God when they were children. Eleven of the thirteen responses had nothing but phrases from choruses and hymns! The hymns we use speak both to us and for us in our faith. The frontier preachers and exhorters needed only two books for their ministry: a Bible and a hymnbook. For them, as for us, the hymnal can be a rich source of spiritual nourishment, second only to the Bible.

Lists of hymns appropriate to the Sunday and its lections may be a helpful starting place, but a list of hymns is no more adequate than a list of Scripture readings! It is the content which can speak to us and for us. Nothing will suffice but "reading" the hymnal over and over again for ourselves. In the process, we can come to a deeper understanding of the nature of our ministry as members of Christ's body. Our ministry, like our use of hymns, is gifted by others. Not many of us are hymn-writers, and even those who are do their work within a heritage already given them. Thus, we do the work of selecting hymns within the framework of gratitude for the legacy we have received.

Insofar as possible, the Scripture lections can help us in making our selection. That reminds us that the Word of God always calls forth our response. This is crucial for the hymns within the Service of the Word. In those services in which there are hymns which can reflect the focus of the Scripture, our worship is greatly empowered. Even more crucial is for the hymn to do what the liturgy at that point of the service is supposed to do. A hymn which is placed in the wrong part of the service is not only ineffective, but also theologically suspect. A valid ministry undertaken at the wrong time suffers in a similar way.

We can become aware that the basic functions hymns serve within the service reflect the nature of our ministry as God's people. Thus, some hymns remind us that we are called to a ministry of praise. A ministry that no longer grows out of a response of praise and thanksgiving will become dull and dry. It is the good news which we proclaim, and only in so far as we know it to be good news for us, will we be able to share the vitality of faith.

We are also ministers of the Word, even as there are hymns of the Word. It is part of the priesthood of all believers to be entrusted with the message of reconciliation.

> Here we are, then, speaking for Christ, as though God himself were making appeal through us. We plead on Christ's behalf: let God change you from enemies into friends! (2 Corinthians 5:20; Adapted from TEV)

Hymns take the message of the Word and proclaim it to us in fresh, new ways. Those words ring in our minds reminding us of the Word of God which has told us we are "ransomed, healed, restored, forgiven."[30] Our ministry responds to that Word through prayer and purpose. Hymns can sing our prayer with a power and depth beyond the spoken word. It is a way in which the Spirit prays for us with sighs deeper than words.

Hymns also affirm that we are a sent-forth people, commissioned to go into all the world, to be the people of God meeting the needs of hurting persons and witnessing to the love of God. As we reflect on the words put together by others out of their life-experiences, our own faith is enriched. Sometimes those words say what we want to say better than we can say it. Sometimes they speak to us the message we need to hear, breaking open the Word of God in new ways, so that we may be nourished and empowered for ministry in Christ's name.

As we prepare for and reflect on the liturgy, we are fed as we discover the resonances between the life of the community and our own spiritual journey in the festivals and seasons of the Church year. Our own sense of identity is developed and enriched as we are shaped by the Word; and we come to a deeper understanding of our ministry through the music we choose. In and through it all, God is at work forming and reforming us to be new creatures in Christ Jesus.

Veni, Sancte Spiritus! Come, Holy Spirit, and form us by the liturgy the work of your people at worship!

Endnotes

1. Summary paraphrase of Alexander Schmemann, *For the Life of the World* (Crestwood, NY: St. Vladimir's Seminary Press, 1973), p. 15.

2. Kevin W. Irwin, *Liturgy, Prayer and Spirituality* (New York: Paulist Press, 1984).

3. Mary Collins, "Critical Questions for Liturgical Theology," *Worship* 53 (July 1977), p. 302.

4. I. H. Dalmais as summarized in Kevin W. Irwin, *Liturgical Theology: A Primer* (Collegeville, MN: The Liturgical Press, 1990) p. 20.

5. David Power, "Unripe Grapes: The Critical Function of Liturgical Theology" in *Worship* 52 (September 1978), p. 399. See also his *Unsearchable Riches: The Symbolic Nature of Liturgy* (Collegeville, MN: Pueblo, 1990).

6. Don E. Saliers, *Worship and Spirituality*, Second ed. (Akron, OH: OSL Publications, 1996), pp. 21-22.

7. For a detailed description of the development of the church year, see Thomas Talley, *Origins of the Liturgical Year* (Pueblo Press, 1986).

8. Adolf Adam, *The Liturgical Year* (New York: Pueblo, 1981), p. 23.

9. Elizabeth Box Price introduced me to the work which she and her husband John had done in integrating the liturgical year with one's personal journey in a workshop at the Christian Educator's Fellowship conference held in Glorietta, New Mexico in the 1970s. Much of what follows is the result of my appropriation of their pioneering work in this regard. Yet it has passed through my own filters and, except where specifically noted, has been recast in my own words.

10. For an excellent translation in contemporary English, see No. 211 in *The United Methodist Hymnal*.

11. John and Elizabeth Box Price, "Spirit Spin," unpublished manuscript.

12. The four Sundays of Advent provide the church with an opportunity to build the sense of joyful expectation in what we see and what we sing. At St. Luke's United Methodist Church in Dubuque, Iowa, which I served as pastor, we followed this pattern: On the first Sunday, we put up a stable — empty except for a few of the animals; a few Advent hangings, and the Advent wreath. On the second Sunday we add the figures of the shepherds with their sheep some distance away from the stable, and add more undecorated greens. On the third Sunday, Mary and Joseph make their appearance placed even farther away, to make their "journey to Bethlehem," and undecorated evergreen trees are added. On the fourth Sunday, the figures of Mary and Joseph are

moved closer to the stable, the figures of the magi are added far to the East (they will "arrive" on Epiphany), and the last of the hangings are added. On Christmas eve, after the Christ candle is lit and the baby is placed in the manger, lights on the trees and the hangings are turned on. White and gold Chrismons may be added to the tree, and the poinsettias put in place (that can also be done on the fourth Sunday, especially if it is near Christmas day). Thus, we move to an increasing mood of joyful expectation, while reserving the "celebration" for the festival itself. In the home, a similar pattern may be developed. Focus on the story through the use of the creche figures is a powerful experience for children and adults alike.

13. Price, op. cit.
14. Ibid.
15. It seems to me, however, that we do not need to deprive those who will attend the services of Maundy Thursday and Good Friday of living through the drama of those events in connection with those holy days. What I have tried to do is to be faithful to the broad outline of the passion story in the gospel for the year, telling the first part of it in its totality, and giving the direction of the story in terms of the Last Supper and the judgement, then stopping the story when Jesus is led away to be crucified. Reference is thus made to the crucifixion — it cannot be escaped by the Sunday-only worshippers, but the details of the story are left for deeper appropriation by those who will live thorough the holy days in their entirety. While that worked for the St. Luke's congregation I served, I do not believe it would be best for all. The pattern must be adapted in terms of the "shape" which the events of holy week take in each congregation.
16. Resources for the Easter Vigil service may be found in Hoyt Hickman et al, *The New Handbook of the Christian Year* (Nashville: Abingdon Press, 1992), pp.191ff. and in *The United Methodist Book of Worship* (Nashville: The United Methodist Publishing House,1992), pp. 369ff. Because the Easter Vigil is being reclaimed in many places, additional resources for other denominations should also be consulted.
17. Price, op. cit.
18. Hickman et al. *The New Handbook of the Christian Year* (*op. cit.*), p. 230. Put your local composer(s) to work on this brief and significant text; then have the whole congregation sing it!
19. Price, op. cit.
20. Leonardo Boff, "Christ's Liberation via Oppression" in *Frontiers of Theology in Latin America*, ed. Rosino Gibellini (Maryknoll, NY: Orbis Books, 1979), p. 130.

21. A recent example can be found in the book edited by Clifton F. Guthrie, *For All the Saints: A Calendar of Commemorations for United Methodists* (Akron, OH: Order of Saint Luke Publications, 1995).

22. Ibid., p. xv.

23. See William Stringfellow, *A Public and Private Faith* (Grand Rapids: William B. Eerdmans Publishing Company, 1962).

24. For a very helpful treatment of the power of scripture in spiritual formation, see the book by M. Robert Mulholland, Jr., *Shaped by the Word* (Nashville: The Upper Room, 1985).

25. See Don Saliers, *Worship and Spirituality* (op. cit.), p. 38.

26. One helpful source is the old *Webster's Collegiate Dictionary*. The copy I have at hand is the fifth edition, published in 1939 by Merriam Company, Springfield, Massachusetts.

27. A phrase most frequently attributed to Isaac Watts.

28. On this bimodal understanding of "service" in worship, see the work of Peter Brunner.

29. My reflection on, and expansion of the title of Alexander Schmemann's seminal book *For the Life of the World*, Second revised edition (Crestwood, NY: St. Vladimir's Seminary Press, 1973).

30. See stanza 1 of "Praise My Soul, the King of Heaven" by Henry F. Lyte.

Nine

Accepting the Call to Service

> . . . and breaking bread from house to house, they shared
> food with glad and generous hearts.
> $\hspace{8cm}$ (Acts 2:46b)
> . . . and [they] distributed to all according to their need.
> $\hspace{8cm}$ (Acts 2:45b)

Nowhere is the demand that liturgical spirituality be related to life clearer than in the question: "Do you accept the call to service?" This is not a question relating to service by the professional ministry, but a call to exercise the general ministry of the people of God.

The call to service involves us in a series of concentric circles. The inner-most circle involves those with whom I live in a covenant relationship: my partner, my covenant prayer group, my religious Order. One makes the decision to answer the call to service in these groups when one joins them. It is in mutual conferring (the often unnoticed meaning in the word *conference!*) that we discern how we may serve one another. Unless there is some over-riding reason to do otherwise, I will heed the call of my mate, my soul-partners, my brothers and sisters in the Order in so far as I am able.

The second circle involves the Church. It is also a covenant community, for the Baptismal Covenant binds us together. I am called on to discern when and where and how I am to serve the Body of Christ. I am not the whole body; I am not called to do everything. But together with others I seek to discern how I can best serve the Church which also serves me.

We are all part of the *apostolate* — those who are sent forth. Where we are sent and how we exercise that apostolate will differ. Discerning what that means for us calls for the use of the means of grace as Wesley

97

identified them: prayer, Scripture, sharing in the Eucharist, and Christian conferring.

The latter may be the great unused resource of liturgical spirituality! Alexander Schmeman observes that Christian liturgy is

> the presence, the actualization in this world of the "world to come" in this *aeon* — of the Kingdom. The mode of this presence, of this actualization of the new life . . . is precisely the *leitourgia*. It is only within this eschatological dimension of the Church that one can understand the nature of the liturgy: to actualize and realize the identity of the *ecclesia* with the new *aeon*, of the "age to come."[1]

So the call to service begins with the prayer: "Thy sovereign rule and realm come; Thy will be done on earth as it is in heaven." And that brings us to the third concentric circle: answering the call to service in the world.

When we offer all we have and are up to God, as we have noted, it is given back to us in a new way and with new responsibility. As Schmemann puts it: "In Christ, life — life in all its totality — was returned to [humanity], given again as sacrament and communion, made Eucharist . . . ."[2] We need to uncover the implications of this for our mission in the world.

That mission is not something restricted to the eschatological future (the time when God's kin-dom is established in its fullness), nor to some grand scheme of the Church universal. Rather, as Kevin Irwin reminds us:

> The eschatological vision of liturgy and life in the world . . . needs to be interpreted in such a way that 'eschatological' does not only mean 'other worldly' [but involves] linking the demands of the kingdom with everyday life.[3]

There is no room for a militant sense of superiority in this call to service — no room for the liturgical *hubris* (pride) which smugly suggests: "we know all about this liturgy stuff, so why don't you let us do it right? You'll just mess it all up!" Rather, as David Power suggests, liturgy fulfills a prophetic function which "calls on all participants to accept the relative and inadequate nature of their own work and compels them to realize that they are always called into question by God's word."[4] Perhaps this is clearer to us when we consider:

Baptism as a Sacrament of Ministry

The laying on of hands links baptism and confirmation with one of the primary symbols of ordination. Baptism is our ordination to the priesthood of all believers. Baptism is a sign of the ministry which we share with all Christians. We affirm together:

> Through Baptism you are incorporated by the Holy Spirit
> into God's new creation and made to share in Christ's royal
> priesthood.[5]

We are confronted with that ministry in the baptismal vows, for the first two questions make the agenda of our ministry unmistakable. The first question asks:

> Do you renounce the spiritual forces of wickedness, reject
> the evil powers of this world, and repent of your sin?

In our spiritual pilgrimage there are certain things we must leave behind, and others things we must reject along the way.

We are called to reject three manifestations of the power of evil: "Sin" as focused on our own lives; the "evil powers of this world" observed all around us. And then, there are the "spiritual forces of wickedness" — those mysterious and unseen, yet none-the-less real powers with which we must contend.

More is needed than rejection and repentance, however. Thus, the second question asks:

> Do you accept the freedom and power God gives you to
> resist evil, injustice, and oppression in whatever forms they
> present themselves?

If the first question asks if we are opposed to what is wrong, the second one asks if we intend to do anything about it. The Baptismal Covenant affirms that God frees us and empowers us to be a part of the "resistance movement."

The ministry of the priesthood of all believers is not restricted to dealing with individual sin, but also with the structures of injustice which oppress human beings. Baptism calls us both to care for individual human beings and to engage in work for a better world in which the rule and realm of God can be manifested.

The ministry to which we are called is symbolized for us in the story of the last supper in John's gospel. We read that

> Jesus poured water into a basin, and began to wash the dis-
> ciples' feet and to wipe them with the towel with which he
> was girded.   (John 13:5)

Whenever the baptismal covenant is celebrated, water is poured and washing takes place. As that happens, we recall that Jesus was involved in servant ministry. We are called to be a "towel and basin" people. Whenever we gather around the font, we need to recall the ministry of love, justice, and service which we share.[6]

In Hebrew there is but one word which we may translate as either "righteousness" or "justice." When in the Baptismal prayer, we pray "clothe them in righteousness," the link with justice is implicit. The problem is that justice usually has to do with various power structures such as business, government, and social class, in as well as out of the church. Whenever we deal with power structures, it is threatening. The powers of this world inevitably want to tell us it is none of our business what they do.

But God is God of all the world, and as the Baptismal Covenant reminds us, Christ has opened the Church "to people of all ages, nations, and races." God cares for all persons; our pledge of allegiance to Jesus Christ affirms more deeply than a pledge of allegiance to a flag that we are committed to liberty and justice for all. The baptismal covenant commissions us to a ministry to justice, for without justice, love is empty.

The baptismal covenant reminds us that because Jesus Christ came to serve we are called to a ministry of service for others. After Jesus took the towel and basin (an action which reminds us of what we do at baptism), he taught them: "I have given you an example; that you should do as I have done to you" (John 13:15). The baptismal covenant reminds us that we are freed to serve others in whatever ways will enable and empower them the most, whether or not we are liked in the process. Through Baptism we are called to be a towel and basin people. As we leave services of the Baptismal Covenant we walk through the *Servant's Entrance* into the world.

Acting in accord with our discipleship

It is clear that the implications for ministries of compassion and of justice are inherent in the words of the Baptismal Covenant. A baptismal spirituality cannot opt out. We are part of Christ's on-going mission as we live into the future. In a baptismal spirituality we seek to open ourselves to being formed by the Holy Spirit as God's reign breaks in and transforms the here and now.

This is not only a Baptismal theme, however; it is also inherent in the Eucharist. In the closing section of the Great Thanksgiving, we become aware that we are nourished in order to minister to others. We pray that "we may be for the world the body of Christ" and that the Spirit will make us "one in ministry to all the world."[7] We are to become the body of Christ in ministry to all the world.

The prayer after communion, coming as it does shortly before the congregation scatters to be the Church in the world, provides an opportunity to make this understanding clear. In Word and Table Service I we pray:

> Grant that we may go into the world in the strength of
> your Spirit, to give ourselves for others, in the name of
> Jesus Christ our Lord.

However, the most powerful expression I know comes in the responsive prayer which balances so well the dialogue with which we begin the Great Thanksgiving:

> You have given yourself to us, Lord.
> **Now we give ourselves for others.**
> Your love has made us a new people;
> **as a people of love we will serve you with joy.**
> Your glory has filled our hearts;
> **Help us glorify you in all things.**[8]

Once again we start with the gift given to us. We are nourished and sustained by the gift of Jesus Christ. But that gift comes in order to prepare us to give ourselves for others as Christ gave himself for us. The love of Christ has made us a new community of persons, called to live in joyful, loving service. The glory of God which fills our lives is to be reflected back in all we do and say and are.

Bread and wine are both given to us in the world of nature, and as a result of human toil and labor. We eat and drink the labor of others. To the extent that their labor is the result of oppression or injustice, we participate in their suffering. What nourishes us is not only the blood of Christ, but the life-blood of others. The broken body and shed blood of Christ were the result of injustice, too.

We break the body. My sociologist colleague, Robert Herrick, once told me that whenever he receives the bread, he rolls it around and squeezes it between his fingers. It is a reminder that it is in our power to do that to other persons, to the Church, to the gift Christ gives us. There should be no way in which we can participate in the Eucharist without a recognition of our call to a ministry of love, justice, and service on behalf of others.

To receive the body and blood of Christ is to become one with him. In one of his post-resurrection appearances, Jesus says to the disciples: "Peace be with you. As the Father has sent me, even so I send you" (John 20:21). Gathered together around the Lord's table, we discover that we are a people bound together in community, that our deepest identity comes from living out our praise and thanksgiving, and that our ministry of service flows from the nourishment we receive.

Veni, Sancte Spiritus! Come, Holy Spirit, and empower us to answer the call to service so that, as we go forth to minister in Christ's name,

"the grace of the Lord Jesus Christ,
    and the love of God,
        and the *koinonia* of the Holy Spirit" goes with us.
            Amen! Let it be so for all of us!

Endnotes

1. Alexander Schmemann, "Theology and Liturgical Tradition" in *Worship In Scripture and Tradition*, Massey H. Shepherd, ed. (New York: Oxford University Press, 1963), p. 171.

2. Alexander Schmemann, *Sacraments and Orthodoxy* (New York: Herder and Herder, 1965), pp. 22-23.

3. Kevin W. Irwin, *Liturgical Theology: A Primer* (Collegeville, MN: The Liturgical Press, 1990) p. 44. Note also the words of Geoffrey Wainwright: "Liturgy has both ethical presuppositions and ethical consequences . . . failure of correspondence between liturgy and ethics amounts to an undesirable separation between the sacred and the secular." *Doxology* (New York: Oxford University Press, 1980), p. 399.

4. David Power, "The Song of the Lord in an Alien Land" in *Politics and Liturgy. Concilium 92*, (New York: Herder and Herder, 1974), p. 105.

5. All references to the ritual are taken from "Baptismal Covenant I" in *The United Methodist Hymnal* (The United Methodist Publishing House, 1989), pp. 33-39.

6. Diaconal ministry in the United Methodist Church involved consecration to these three areas of ministry. That commitment ought to remind us that, as a church, we are called to be a diaconal people — a servant people, called to respond through love, justice, and service to the world around us.

7. References to the eucharistic liturgy are taken from "A Service of Word and Table I" in *The United Methodist Hymnal*, pp. 6-11.

8. *The Book of Services*, p. 45.

Ten

Seeking Meaning to Nourish Our Souls:
TOWARD A THEOLOGY OF LITURGICAL SPIRITUALITY

When I look back at the pilgrimage we have shared in the preceding pages, a framework of meaning emerges which may help us understand that journey. For some, it is enough to be able to "talk the talk" and "walk the walk." But my calling to academic vocation makes it impossible for me to be satisfied with that. I need to share with you — at least those of you who also have this propensity for seeking frameworks of meaning — the assumptions behind the explorations of the preceding chapters.

I am convinced that our spirituality is nourished through roots which are earlier and deeper than the experiences we recall. The matrix of meaning for our lives is dynamic and organic. It not only resides in our consciousness, but arises out of the fabric of our existence. We have seen how corporate experiences of worship and the rhythm of daily prayer have the potential of making transparent what may appear to be common and ordinary, so that we discover reservoirs of spiritual meaning and nourishment of which we were aware only dimly.

We have discovered that liturgical events have potential out of which we can sculpt meaning, and we have insisted that spiritual nourishment and meaning sculpting can be integrally related for persons of faith through liturgy. In reflecting on the celebration of the sacraments, for example, we found the ordinary invested with significant meaning through which God feeds us. In baptism ordinary water becomes quite extraordinary. Whenever we celebrate the baptismal covenant, we can receive spiritual nourishment and meaning.

In developing a theology of liturgical spirituality we find in liturgical events symbols which are both soul-nourishing and meaning-sculpting. They help us confront some of the most basic questions with which we must wrestle on our life pilgrimage: Where do we belong? Who are we? What are we doing here? Liturgy (perhaps most clearly in the sacraments, though not only there) speaks to us and for us about belonging, identity, and ministry. Thus, to remember our baptism is not merely to recall an event in the past. It is to appropriate in the present what it means to live out our baptism.

Liturgical theology asks: how are *lex orandi* (the rule of prayer), and *lex credendi* (the rule of belief) related?[1] We might frame a similar question this way: how is our life of prayer and worship related to our search for meaning — a search which involves our believing and our thinking.

There are three possible approaches. One is that prayer, especially public liturgical word/acts, grounds belief.[2] In this view, the affirmation "You are my God" is more basic to belief in the existence of God than are philosophical arguments or theological expositions on the nature of God. Rather, the latter involve the reflection of human intellect on religious experience. Thus, my theological mentor Nels Ferre contended that Christian theologizing starts out on its knees!

The methodology of liturgical theology from this perspective sees liturgy as a resource for doing theology. The historical influence of liturgical language and practice upon creeds, confessions, and theological perspectives needs to be described. Our search for meaning, then, needs to look to the liturgy for insights and perspectives which will help us in that task.

A second approach is that belief grounds prayer.[3] After all, prayer and worship involve the implicit assumption that there is a God. In this approach to seeking meaning, both theological affirmations and theological presuppositions present in liturgy are identified, and then tested against and judged by the theological affirmations of the liturgical community. This view recognizes that our prayer and worship function within presuppositions (sometimes explicit, but always implicit) about the nature of reality and how and to what degree we are able to know it.

How do we handle the recognition that there is truth in both these approaches when they seem contradictory? A third approach is that there is a mutual interrelationship between prayer and belief.[4] The "cause and effect" analysis implied by the first two approaches is inadequate. There are times when liturgy is the source out of which theological affirmation arises and other times when liturgies are created to reflect theological affirmations. An approach is needed which will overcome the dichotomy. As Dietrich Ritschl has observed:

> Nature and grace, reason and faith, scholarship and piety, theology and doxology, historical past and existential present have been separated from each other.[5]

They need to be reunited. Those seeking to develop a theology of liturgi-cal spirituality are called to engage in that task.

Not only are liturgy and theology interactive, however. There is an important sense in which prayer and liturgy are themselves theology. Gerard Lukken reminds us that

> the first meaning of "orthodoxy" was also right praise (*ortho-doxia*) in the liturgy and it is only in the secondary, derived sense that it came to mean right teaching.[6]

Observation makes clear that worship involves words to and about God. Such speech is theological. But there is a deeper sense in which we may understand liturgy as a theological act.

Theology is not a term which is restricted to reflecting on language which directly refers to God. Even a quick glance at the contents of books which purport to be about theology shows that a wider meaning of the term is being assumed. Indeed, a wide variety of topics may be discussed, but they are seen as being interrelated. They all, in some way or another, take "God" (whether understood as "Absolute," "Transcendent," or even "limited") into account in the process. Theologizing, then, has to do with sculpting a matrix of meanings which is related both to our understanding of God and to the ways in which we are nourished on our journey.

We have been seeking a matrix of meaning in a Lukan perspective on liturgical spirituality and the sacramental life. What have been the marks, the characteristics of our "liturgical theologizing" — for while we have not named it that, that is what we have been doing!

Our insistence on the importance of the paschal mystery in this ap-proach to liturgical theologizing reminds us that a theology of liturgical spirituality is *kerygmatic*. That is, it is rooted in the proclamation of the Christian story which centers in the Christ event. Our resources for un-covering what is at the heart of that ongoing proclamation are found in Scripture and tradition, and you have seen that I believe they must be taken seriously. How we use them, how we go about appropriating, inter-preting and applying them are what we call *hermeneutical questions*. Taylor McConnell observes that while we tend to think of stories as functioning to "illustrate" a concept, he has come to believe that "stories are the es-sence of theological thinking" while "propositional statements are the skeleton or outline of them."[7] Liturgical theologizing seeks to identify the points at which the Story and our liturgical experience intersect with our stories so as to provide meaning and nourishment for us.

Such theologizing is also *doxological*; that is, it is done from the perspective of the praise of the living God. The labor we expend on sculpting meaning is dependent on the giftedness of life, and the nourishment of the Holy Spirit comes as grace. This does not imply that it comes easily or that it is always pleasant. Critical analysis is indispensable but it must be balanced with critical appropriation. The identification of ways in which our theologizing has been insensitive, and where it has been used as a tool of oppression cannot be ignored. Getting rid of the "dead wood" clears the way for new growth. Liturgical theologizing must return again and again to the recognition that all its work is surrounded by the one in whom "we live and move and have our being" [Acts 17:28].

At the same time, we have been discovering that this kind of liturgical theologizing is also *ecclesial*; it takes place within the context of the Church. It is not a game of mental solitaire. It is not merely a reflection of my ponderings and perplexities. As II Corinthians 4:5 says, we are called to proclaim not ourselves, but Jesus Christ as Lord.

We are entrusted with the faith of the Church. What I believe as an individual is important to my meaning sculpting and soul nourishing. In my personal theologizing, I seek to work it out carefully and clearly. But I must see it in light of the larger community of faith, and I must take the testimony of that community seriously in working out my own appropriations of it.

In the end, both meaning and nourishment are essentially communal in nature. I am nourished by that which is beyond myself as it is processed by what is within myself. Meaning seeks to transcend the split between personal and communal horizons — not with the object of eradicating either one but by enabling communication (note the presence of "*commun*" in both *commun*al and *commun*ication!).

It is not a question of whether the theology of liturgical spirituality should be an individual or corporate activity. It is a task for individuals-in-community and for communities-of-individuals. That is also the way in which we must understand the nature of the Church. James Gustafson helps us recognize that the Church shares language, interpretation, memory, and action. Through means such as these, we are enabled to appropriate the lived experience of the past so that it becomes our own lived experience. In this process, the communication of significant symbols is crucial.[8] A theology of liturgical spirituality is based on the communication of significant symbols in the worship of the Church.

However, we must be aware of horizons which go beyond the Church. The approach we have taken to liturgical theologizing here is also *contextual*. We learn the importance of that in the study of Scripture itself. In understanding a text, we are helped by knowing its *sitz-im-leben*, its situation in life. Jeremiah's buying a field becomes a prophetic act only when we know that the nation is facing defeat, and that purchasing property which was part of the covenant with God is an affirmation that God will not forsake that covenant even in defeat. The opening words of John's gospel: ("in the beginning was the WORD, the *LOGOS*") takes a term from Hellenistic Judaic philosophy and interprets the Incarnation by transfiguring its terminology. Luke's life situation in a Church in which the inclusion of Gentiles is being actualized is reflected in the way he sees both Jesus and the early Church.

Both Old and New testaments, then, contain examples of theologizing as contextual. This is true for events as well as texts. The temptation, not only in studying Scripture, but in all hermeneutical endeavors, is to take *our* cultural context and pour everything else into its mold. Not only is this intellectually dishonest, however; it is also an act which impoverishes us.

On the other hand, not to recognize the context out of which we operate does not make it go away, but only exert hidden influence. In the theologizing I do, my own context as a United Methodist who has found nourishment in the resources of my denomination is evident. In teaching and writing, I invite those who share other contexts to seek parallels within their own experience. Theologizing is always done from a given standpoint, but that does not mean that the meaning it sculpts has meaning only from within that standpoint. The fusion of horizons, of which Gademer speaks, is a part of all communication.[9]

The relationship between this understanding of theology and the liturgy is implicit in Alexander Schmemann's assertion that "liturgical theology is the elucidation of the meaning of worship."[10] Such a definition carries with it the assumption that worship already has *a* meaning. It is more accurate for me to speak of the *matrix of meanings* which are there, and to recognize that participation in liturgical events involves us in the meaning-sculpting process, both as a community of individuals and as individuals in that community.

Gordon Lathrop's liturgical theology assumes something akin to this perspective. He contends that to inquire into the *ordo* [the "shape of the liturgy" through the ages] is "to inquire about the way 'meaning' occurs in Christian worship."[11] Elements of this meaning are in fact "given to us" or "discovered" through participation in the liturgy. These elements are themselves the product of the sculpting of meaning by earlier communities of faith. But the matrix of meaning in the liturgy is not something static waiting to be discovered. We must enter into the creative process through which significant meaning becomes the source of our spiritual nourishment.

In understanding how this takes place, Lathrop joins others in drawing a helpful distinction between "primary liturgical theology" which has to do with sacred objects, words, places, times and peoples, and "secondary liturgical theology" which has to do with the patterns of the liturgy which he sees exemplified in the juxtaposition of ancient things and new hope.[12]

If we are to engage in that kind of theologizing, we must understand what is at stake in the interpretive task. What hermeneutical perspectives assist us in developing a theology of liturgical spirituality?

One dimension of our work will involve a hermeneutic of remembrance or *anamnesis*.[13] This interpretive methodology seeks to reconstruct meaning by identifying and reflecting on images from past traditions which are still appropriate. In the process, earlier insights which have been forgotten or obscured may be reclaimed. We may be able to recognize parallels which have gone unnoticed.

Another dimension of our work involves a hermeneutic of suspicion. The origin of liturgical texts, symbols and actions, as well as the tradition of their interpretation are influenced by social location and interest. So are those of us who undertake the task of developing a theology of liturgical spirituality. Therefore, we must identify and be critical about the way in which cultural context influences what we are doing. As Ruth Duck puts it:

> It requires that one's presuppositions and social commitments be made as consciously as possible, enabling self-criticism and honest hearing. At the same time, through this hermeneutic, one may criticize past traditions and refuse to appropriate them in present thinking and practice.[14]

A third facet of the task involves a hermeneutic of dynamic equivalence.[15] This approach seeks to uncover the various meanings and references of a liturgical act and translate those meanings into equivalents which are more illuminating than a strict parallel might be. Thus we would seek to identify language and symbols which perform parallel (though often not identical) functions in the contemporary context.

The danger here, as in Biblical translation, is that this approach can be used to justify inaccurate subjective interpretation. It is also possible, however, for it to be a rigorous examination of the transfer of meanings which seeks to avoid both adding to or subtracting from traditional interpretations in ways which do not violate but rather illuminate liturgical spirituality.

I would suggest a fourth methodology which grows out of the dynamic equivalence approach. We might call it a hermeneutic of creative contextualization (literally, *with* the text), and it may be particularly relevant to the development of a theology of liturgical spirituality.[16] This approach recognizes contributions from the history of the tradition. It also seeks to understand and appropriate the significance of liturgical experiences for spirituality in new and creative ways out of the "surplus of meaning" in those experiences. In so doing, we are able to acknowledge and name concerns arising out of our immediate context. Lathrop talks about the way in which liturgical texts move "toward speaking a thing greater than they have contained." As such they become a "new thing" which is a "word of grace beyond words that transforms and destroys and saves our old practice."[17]

One historical example of this is what goes on when we take the Isaiah texts and place them in context of Advent. In that context the Church has found it appropriate to apply them to the coming of Jesus. Earlier interpretations tended to talk these texts being "fulfilled" (thereby, seeming to imply a prediction/vindication pattern). In the Advent context, however, it may be more accurate to talk about those texts as being "filled-full" of significant meaning by appropriating them in light of the coming celebration of the Incarnation. For the early Church they became "words of grace" which transformed the old meanings, "destroying" some earlier interpretations (which may indeed be more accurate for understanding the situation-in-life of the original con-text).

It is not primarily the text which is transformed, however. It is the liturgical event of an Advent people who sculpt meaning for their lives out of the spiritual nourishment they receive. This approach recognizes that the context out of which we come will discover certain questions and answers in liturgical experience which are both soul nourishing and meaning-sculpting for us. We are able to engage liturgy in a dialog which seeks a fusion of horizons. The "breaking open" of liturgical experience in new ways comes out of both the context in which a particular liturgical action originated and developed and the context of the contemporary participants.

In the eighth chapter of Acts there is an account of an Ethiopian eunuch struggling with sculpting meaning and receiving spiritual nourishment. A particular text provides the occasion for this struggle, but the eunuch's need is not for a translator of the text but for a contemporary contextualization which speaks living truth. In the presence of that kind of engagement, baptism is invested with immediate meaning and significance.

The answer to the eunuch's question: "how can I understand unless someone explain it to me?" is in part answered by Philip's contextualizing the passage in terms of the good news of Jesus Christ. But it is only as the Ethiopian existentially appropriates that teaching that understanding takes place. In that regard, the "someone" in the Ethiopian's question, I am convinced, was finally not Philip but the Holy Spirit, fusing the horizons of the writer of the text, the interpreter, and the Ethiopian. In a similar manner, a theology of liturgical spirituality seeks to fuse the horizons of those who developed liturgical actions (including texts, spoken and sung words, sign-acts, and their larger liturgical context), the traditions which have conserved and transmitted those actions, and those who share in those experiences today.

Spiritual nourishment and meaning-sculpting are integrally related for persons of faith. It is our task to provide sign-posts which may be helpful as disciples-in-community today seek to creatively appropriate the living Word which God has spoken, is speaking, and will speak. What I have written in these pages is not meant to provide final answers, but to serve as a catalyst for persons who share these concerns. Seeking a Lukan perspective on liturgical spirituality and the sacramental life is an on-going task. That is why we pray: *Veni, Sancte Spiritus!* Come, Holy Spirit, and open us to the transcendent promptings of your grace. In the words of the great thirteenth century hymn:

> Come, Holy Spirit, come;
> Radiate your light divine.
> Source of all gifts, come;
> Shine within our hearts.

> Great Comforter,
> The soul's most welcome guest:
> In labor you are rest,
> In heat, coolness,
> In woe, reassurance and relief.

O blessed Light,
Shine within our hearts and fill our inmost being.
Without you, nothing is free from taint of ill,
Nothing is good in thought or deed.
Heal what is wounded,
Strengthen what is weak,
Cleanse what is filthy,
Water what is parched,
Bend what is stubborn,
Melt what is frozen,
Warm what is chill,
Guide what is devious.
On the faithful who trust in you,
Pour out your sevenfold gifts;
Give us boundless mercy--
Your salvation--
Joy unending.
Amen.[18]

ENDNOTES

1. This Latin phrase has been used as a convenient shorthand for the more complete statement attributed to Prosper of Aquitaine,   c. 435: *legem credendi lex statuat supplicandi* which refers in its original context to Good Friday intercessions. "Prosper's point . . . is that in asking that God's grace come to various groups of people, the Church asserts her belief (against the Pelagians) that it is grace and not works that leaders to salvation." (Kevin Irwin, *Liturgical Theology: A Primer* [Collegeville: The Liturgical Press, 1990], pp. 11-12.)

2. See, for example, the writing of Aiden Kavanagh, *On Liturgical Theology* (Collegeville, MN: Pueblo Publishing Company, 1984). This view is captured in the title of the book by Leonel L. Mitchell, *Praying Shapes Believing* (Minneapolis, MN: Winston Press, 1985).

3. This position is developed by Geoffrey Wainwright. See, for example, *Doxology: The Praise of God in Worship, Doctrine, and Life* (New York: Oxford University Press, 1980).

4. For example, see the work of Alexander Schmemann, e.g. *Introduction to Liturgical Theology* (Crestwood, NY: St. Vladimir's Seminary Press, 1986).

5. Dietrich Ritschl, *Memory and Hope* (New York: Macmillan, 1966), p. xiii.

6. Gerard Lukken, "The Unique Expression of Faith in the Liturgy" *Liturgical Expression of Faith, Concilium 82*, David Smith, trans. (New York: Herder and Herder, 1973), p. 63.

7. Taylor and June McConnell, *Research Report 005* (Garrett-Evangelical Theological Seminary: Bureau of Social and Religious Research, n.d.), p.32.

8. James Gustafson, *Treasure in Earthen Vessels: The Church as a Human Community* (New York: Harper and Brothers, 1961). Cf. also Edward Farley's discussion of "distinctive intersubjectivity" in *Ecclesial Man: A Social Phenomenology of Faith and Reality* (Philadelphia: Fortress Press, 1975), chapters 4-7.

9. For an overview, see "The Historicity of Understanding" by Hans-Georg Gadamer in Kurt Mueller-Vollmer, ed., *The Hermeneutics Reader* (New York: Continuum, 1989), pp. 256-291.

10. Alexander Schmemann, *Introduction to Liturgical Theology*, p. 16.

11. Gordon Lathrop, "Holy Things: Foundations for Liturgical Theology" in *Foundations: Renewing Parish Worship*, Institute of Liturgical Studies Occasional Papers, Number 7 (Valparaiso: Institute of Liturgical·Stud-

ies, 1991), p. 21. This approach is developed more completely in *Holy Things: A Liturgical Theology* (Minneapolis, MN: Fortress Press, 1993).

12. This pattern is described in the Introduction to Lathrop's book, *Holy Things: A Liturgical Theology*, pp. 1-11.

13. See the discussion in Ruth C. Duck, *Gender and the Name of God: The Trinitarian Baptismal Formula* (New York: Pilgrim Press, 1991), pp. 89ff.

14. Ibid., p. 87.

15. The phrase comes from Eugene Nida and was used to describe an approach to Biblical translation, but it is appropriate for liturgical hermeneutics as well. Cf. *Toward a Science of Translating* (Leiden: E. J. Brill, 1964).

16. In developing liturgies themselves, Ruth Duck speaks of "the method of creative ritualization." (*op. cit.*, pp. 100-107).

17. Gordon Lathrop, "Holy Things: Foundations for Liturgical Theology" in *Institute of Liturgical Studies Occasional Papers*, Number 7, (Randall R. Lee and David G. Truemper, eds, Valparaiso, IN: Institute of Liturgical Studies, 1991), pp. 8-9. Cf. also Lathrop's book, *Holy Things: A Liturgical Theology*.

18. Adapted by DWV from the thirteenth century prayer of Archbishop Stephen Langton as translated by E. Caswall (1814-1878); Adapted from *The Daily Office: A Book of Hours for Daily Prayer After the Use of the Order of Saint Luke*, copyright 1994 by the Order of Saint Luke. Used by permission.

Appendix A

THE RULE OF LIFE AND SERVICE OF THE ORDER OF SAINT LUKE

is a primary means of spiritual formation by which all members covenant to live. Each member vows to abide by this Rule and to indicate their commitment by study, service, gifts and practice.

WE AFFIRM THE APOSTOLIC HOPE With the apostles and the Church through the ages, we affirm Jesus Christ, Sacrament of the presence of God, as the source of our hope. We take our name from St Luke the Evangelist, and seek to be incorporated into the paschal mystery he proclaims. We pray that we may be formed by the incarnation, life, death, resurrection, ascension, gift of the Holy Spirit and coming again of Jesus Christ. We are sent forth to proclaim and to live the hope that good news brings.

WE LIVE FOR THE CHURCH OF JESUS CHRIST We believe that the Church is the Body of Christ and we are called to worship, learning, community and service as members of that Body. We affirm our fidelity to oneness in Christ in the Church truly catholic, truly apostolic, truly evangelical, and truly reformed which supercedes all division by denomination, and which we believe God will gather together from a broken Christendom. Our apostolic mission includes calling the Church to liturgical and sacramental renewal, and seeking to bring the healing grace of Christ to all Creation.

WE SEEK THE SACRAMENTAL LIFE We are called to become aware of God's presence through eucharistic living. We seek to live out our baptism into Christ's death and resurrection. We receive with gratitude all that God has given us and offer it up to God. We receive it again from

God transformed to use for the sake of the world. We join the Church through the ages and around the world in recognizing that all time is in God's hands. As we faithfully pray the Daily Office, and live so as to embody our prayers, we endeavor to live the sacramental life. By so doing, we seek to be formed as a means of grace for all those we meet and serve in Christ's name.

WE PROMOTE THE CORPORATE WORSHIP OF THE CHURCH

We believe that the corporate worship of the Church is liturgy- the work of the people on behalf of all creation- which is our response to the revelation of God's grace. Through our collective memory and our shared hope, the Holy Spirit acts in Word and Sacrament making present to us the saving acts of God and transforming us so that we can be God's people. Through our worship, we seek the glorification of God and the sanctification of the Church. This worship is offered in the name of the community which claims it as the manifestation of its own identity and mission. We seek to encourage the Church to worship with vitality and integrity, appropriating the rites and services of the Church, historically and ecumenically grounded, which enable us to worship together in the name of Jesus Christ. We honor the worship traditions of the past and seek to be open to new ways of expressing the heritage of faith they embody in ways that speak to us and for us in the present. We witness to the saving and transforming work of God which renews us in Christ's body, the Church, through the continual offering up of our lives to God.

WE MAGNIFY THE SACRAMENTS

We believe that the sacraments are Christ's gift to the Church. Individually and corporately we are called to lift up these mysteries in the life of the Church as means of grace through which we are formed as Christian disciples. Through the baptismal covenant, we are incorporated into the death and resurrection of Jesus Christ. God calls us to live out the redemptive, liberating, justice-seeking ministry of Jesus. We seek to deepen our understanding, and the understanding of the Church, of the significance of the baptismal covenant and the Eucharist for Christian discipleship and service. We believe that the Eucharist re-presents the life-gift of Jesus Christ in which the living spirit of Christ is truly present to us, preserving and reforming Christ's Body, the Church. Frequent celebration of the Eucharist forms us in the sacramental life empowering us to become Christ's healing presence in the world.

WE ACCEPT THE CALL TO SERVICE

By virtue of our baptism, God calls each of us to ministries which are a proclamation of Christ, seeking wholeness for Creation. Through sacramental, prophetic and pastoral ministries we turn in openness and love to the world. We identify with the whole community of humankind, especially those who live on the margins, and invite people to touch our lives as we touch theirs. Thus we may all know the perfect joy of being reconciled with God. In community with our brothers and sisters, we seek to discern the ways in which we are called to serve God in the Order, the Church and the world.

Appendix B
Accountability: To Whom? For What?
The Ongoing Challenge for Spirituality

Covenant-making is part of our social fabric. We participate in it when partners pledge their love, when persons are baptized and become members of the church, when we buy or rent a house, write a check, use a charge card, or get a driver's license. From the central activities of life to the mundane, covenant-making pervades our human experience.

Covenants made are not always covenants kept, however. There are divorces, foreclosures, canceled credit ratings, and that group of folks we call the "lapsed baptized." Perhaps some enter into covenants knowing they will be broken, but for most of us most of the time, we enter into a covenant in "good faith" believing that we and those with whom we join will do our best to keep the covenant we have made.

There are problems, there can be no question. Sometimes we do not know "what we were getting ourselves into." Sometimes we "get in over our heads." Sometimes we discover that the value of the covenant is not what we expected. With the best sense of honor and integrity we can muster, we find ways to terminate the covenant.

There are those for whom a covenant ceases to have any meaning at all, and so life is lived as though the covenant did not exist even when it is not formally canceled.

What of the rest of us? We take the covenants we have made (whether with our partner, our church, or a religious order) seriously. The vows we make are statements of intention, and we do not take them lightly. Yet we discover that keeping the covenant is not easy. We begin to ponder what the vows really mean. What seemed relatively clear when we began turns out to have all kinds of complexities we had not expected. In addition, we discover that we have an amazing tendency to rationalize to ourselves why we are not doing what we intended to do.

How do we sort out the difference between our legitimate pondering of perplexities, and "letting ourselves off the hook" too easily? How do we deal with our human need for accountability?

As an example, we might reflect on what happens when members of the Order of Saint Luke covenant to seek the sacramental life. The "Rule of Life and Service" of the Order indicates that one component of that vow involves praying the Daily Office. What does that mean? Does it mean praying seven offices a day seven days a week three hundred and sixty-five days a year? Does it mean praying Morning and Evening prayer every day? Does it mean praying some part of the office some days? Or does it mean that I have covenanted that I will spend some time in prayer each day? How can I reflect on what it means? How can I be helped to "grow into" the covenant I have made?

One approach is to make the expectations as specific as possible. The General Chapter of the Order might decide that the covenant to pray the Daily Office implies that one will spend at least one hour each day using the resources for the Daily Office provided by the Order; or that one will pray Morning or Evening prayer at least six times a week; or that one should use at least one of the offices each day. This is sometimes a helpful approach. It gives us clear and concise guidance about what it means to keep our covenant. But not everyone has the same needs. Not every one is fed in the same way. What is significant at one time in my life may be merely rote observance at another time.

It may be helpful for groups of persons who share a similar vision to set some common expectations. They could enter into a covenant with each other about those expectations, becoming accountable to one another for them, but recognizing that not all who have taken similar vows will understand them in the same way.

Another approach is to have a group of people who meet regularly talk through the covenant and come up with a common set of expectations for a given period of time. For example, a chapter might decide that during Lent all members will pray the Evening Prayer office, or that they will have an overnight retreat at which they will pray all seven offices. In this way, community becomes the context for accountability. We set our expectations together and then reflect together on how we have followed through — what nourishment we have received and what problems we have encountered. We help feed one another.

A third approach to accountability has its roots in the practice of an individual having a "confessor" or a "spiritual companion." There is a long history in religious orders for the role of a confessor for everyone from abbot to novice. Here there is a recognition that as individuals, we must think through our own accountability in terms of their own journey, but that it will be more helpful if we don't do it alone. Discernment can emerge as we share with each other where we are on our journey: where we are moving on; where we are on a plateau; where we are backsliding; and, more importantly, why? Is it that our needs have changed? Is it that different disciplines have supplanted earlier practices? Or have I just become weary in well-doing?

Talking with a spiritual companion about what it means for me to pray the Daily Office may result in a recognition that when I have good resources and develop a pattern I follow it with some consistency. We may discover as we talk together that when the pattern is broken it is hard to re-establish. I may covenant with my companion that I will strive to pray Morning and Evening Prayer as often as possible. When I discover I haven't done that, I will pray Compline. And when I get in bed and remember I've done none of the above, I will pray the commendation for the night and the Song of Simeon, not as a replacement for the Daily Office but as a reminder to myself that I have *not* prayed it, but knowing that others *have* prayed it, and that on other days I *will* pray it *for them*.

These examples relate to only one part of one of the vows of the Order of Saint Luke, but they illustrate some of the ways in which we can seek to be accountable, whether or not we are members of an order. One road to accountability is the willingness to arrange things so I can say each year; "Yes, I have reflected with another pilgrim on the journey about the nature of my own pilgrimage. I have tried to be honest with that person, and to have them help me discern where I need to be going. We have prayed together about it, and now I can go forward knowing I am not alone."

GUIDES FOR MEDITATION AND REFLECTION

Note: These guides for meditation and reflection are provided for chapters one through nine, and Appendix B on "accountability." They may be used by pilgrims individually or in community, at home or on retreat.

Seeking a Lukan Spirituality (Chapter One)
1. *Prayer for Illumination*
For your prayers today, pray all three of the "gospel canticles" — the Song of Mary (Luke 1:46-55), the Song of Zechariah (Luke 1:68-79), and the Song of Simeon (Luke 2:29-32). Take your time and let them pray through you.

2. *Listening for the Word of God*
Continue to reflect on these three canticle passages, and also read Acts 2:42 and 46-47. "Brood" over the passages, and let them grasp you. Ponder their meaning for your spirituality and that of your covenant partners.

3. *Reflection*
Start by asking these questions, and see what the Spirit leads you to think about as you do!

How does Luke's emphasis on the work of the Spirit help us understand the nature of the spirituality we seek?

What is the "good news" to which Luke witnesses?

Which of the "markers to guide our journey" are calling you to greater accountability?

How can we begin to "live into" a Lukan spirituality?

4. *Prayer*
In your prayer time, or as part of praying the Daily Office or celebrating the Eucharist, include the *Veni, Sancte Spiritus* found on page iii.

121

Affirming the Apostolic Hope (Chapter Two)

1. Prayer for Illumination
Pray that you will be able to identify your own deep hunger for God and discover the apostolic hope as a resource that nourishes your most authentic self.

2. Listening for the Word of God
Read Psalm 42.
"Brood" over the passage, letting words, phrases, or ideas grasp you. Ponder their meaning for you.

When you have identified the ways in which you thirst for God, read Ephesians 2:11-23.

Live with its message about the apostolic hope in prayerful   dialogue.

3. Reflection
You may find it helpful to write down the ways in which you find yourself being addressed by God in these passages and/or to discuss it with others.

Be open both to insights which witness to the Spirit at work within you, and to those insights which call you to account. Include your questions, frustrations and feelings as they surface.

4. Prayer
In your prayer time, or as part of praying the Daily Office or celebrating the Eucharist, include the *Veni, Sancte Spiritus* found on page iii.

Being the Church of Jesus Christ (Chapter Three)

1. Prayer for Illumination
Think of the ways in which the Church has been a channel of grace for you. Set aside for the moment the times when you have been hurt or disappointed or angry because of what churches have done or not done. Let the Spirit stir up within you thanksgiving to God for the community of faith past and present who are Christ's Body to and for and with you.

2. *Listening for the Word of God*
Read 1 Peter 2:9-10 and 1 Corinthians 12:27-31.
Note that the latter passage is what leads into 1 Corinthians 13! What does that say about the nature of the Church? "Brood" over these passages, letting words, phrases, or ideas grasp you. Ponder their meaning for you.

Live with these passages in prayerful dialogue.

3. *Reflection*
You may find it helpful to write down the ways in which you find yourself being addressed by God in these passages and/or to discuss it with others.

Be open both to insights which witness to the Spirit at work within you, and to those insights which call you to account. Include your questions, frustrations and feelings as they surface.

4. *Prayer*
In your prayer time, or as part of praying the Daily Office or celebrating the Eucharist, include the *Veni, Sancte Spiritus* found on page iii.

Magnifying the Sacraments (Chapter Four)

1. *Prayer for Illumination*
Pray that you will be open to hear the word God has for you today. You might symbolize this by first clenching your fists, holding them palms down on your lap. Slowly open them, releasing anything you are holding back into God's keeping. Then turn them over, holding them with palms up and open, indicating that you are ready to receive whatever God wants to give you. Don't hurry through this preparation; take time to "center down" in the presence of God.

2. *Listening for the Word of God*
Read 1 Peter 2:9-10, Romans 6:3-11, and Colossians 2:6-7. "Brood" over each passage, letting words, phrases, or ideas grasp you. Ponder their meaning. Let them begin to pray through you.

3. *Reflection*
You may find it helpful to write down the ways in which you find yourself being addressed by God. Be open both to insights which witness to the Spirit at work within you, and to those which call you to account. In

clude your questions, longings, doubts, and frustrations, as they come to mind. Don't be concerned about a "finished product" — just let the thoughts flow.

The following questions may be helpful, but don't be limited by them or feel obligated to use them if something else is being dealt with which is more important for you.

1. What can baptism say to me about my "place of belonging?" How does renewal of my baptism help me deal with my frustrations with the church?

2. What can baptism say to me about who I am? How does the Spirit of God help me understand my identity through baptism?

3. What would it mean for me to live a "eucharistic" life? How is God calling me to respond in and through the sacrament to the implications for my ministry?

4. Prayer
In your prayer time, or as part of praying the Daily Office or celebrating the Eucharist, include the Veni, Sancte Spiritus found on page iii.

Seeking the Sacramental Life   (Chapter Five)

1. Prayer for Illumination
Put yourself in the presence of the beauty of the creation, either actually or in your imagination. Let God open the eyes of your soul so that beyond the natural objects you recognize the Transcendent One toward whom they point. Let them become channels of God's grace to you. Don't hurry through this preparation; take time to become aware of the living presence of God.

2. Listening for the Word of God
Read Psalm 104. "Brood" over it, letting words, phrases, or ideas grasp you. Ponder their meaning.

3. Reflection
Ask yourself: How can I appropriate the sacramentality of creation more fully? What can I do to become more aware of the sacramentality of time?

4. Prayer
In your prayer time, or as part of praying the Daily Office or celebrating the Eucharist, include the *Veni, Sancte Spiritus* found on page iii.

Baptismal Spirituality (Chapter Six)

1. Prayer for Illumination
Place some water on your forehead, your eyes, your mouth, your ears, your heart. Each time say: "I am baptized! Thanks be to God!"

2. Listening for the Word of God
Read Romans 6:3-11. "Brood" over it, letting words, phrases, or ideas grasp you. Ponder their meaning.

3. Reflection
Ask yourself: What does it mean for me today to live out my baptism? Let the Holy Spirit probe deeply as you reflect on your first answers and try to get beneath them or to find within them the Word God has for you today.

4. Prayer
In your prayer time, or as part of praying the Daily Office or celebrating the Eucharist, include the *Veni, Sancte Spiritus* found on page iii.

The Spirituality of the Pastoral Offices (Chapter Seven)

1. Prayer for Illumination
Lift up in prayer persons you know who have experienced the pastoral offices recently. Then ask the Holy Spirit to teach you through these offices.

2. Listening for the Word of God
Read Psalm 23. Listen for the resonances with the pastoral office. Ponder its meaning.

3. *Reflection*
Ask yourself: Where am I in my spiritual life right now in regard to these pastoral offices? Of which am I in need? Which do I fear? What do I learn when I share in them with others? What can I do to become more aware of the sacramentality they provide? of time?

4. *Prayer*
In your prayer time, or as part of praying the Daily Office or celebrating the Eucharist, include the *Veni, Sancte Spiritus* found on page iii.

Participating in the Corporate Worship of the Church
(Chapter Eight)

1. *Prayer for Illumination*
Think of a prayer which you associate with the worship of the church. It might be a collect, such as the Collect for Purity ("Almighty God unto whom all hearts are open . . .") or even the Lord's Prayer. Pray that prayer, being aware that you do not pray it alone, but as a part of the whole Church through the ages and around the world.

2. *Listening for the Word of God*
Read Luke 24: 13-35. Are there ways in which it is like what the worship of the church is for you? "Brood" over it, letting words, phrases, or ideas grasp you. Ponder their meaning.

3. *Reflection*
Ask yourself: What season of the church year am I in right now? How does naming it that way help me understand both myself and the season involved?

4. *Prayer*
In your prayer time, or as part of praying the Daily Office or celebrating the Eucharist, include the *Veni, Sancte Spiritus* found on page iii.

Accepting the Call to Service   (Chapter Nine)

1. *Prayer for Illumination*
Pray that the Spirit will enable you to remove the "static" and distortion from your communication with God.

Hold your Bible in your hands as if it were a gift with your name on it. Give thanks for it, and open it with expectation and anticipation.

Don't hurry through this preparation; take time to become aware of the living presence of God.

2. Listening for the Word of God
Read John 13:1-15 and 1 John 4:7-12.
"Brood" over each passage, letting words, phrases, or ideas grasp you. Ponder their meaning.

3. Reflection
You may find it helpful to write down the ways in which you find yourself being addressed by God in these passages. Be open both to insights which witness to the Spirit at work within you, and to those which call you to account. Include your questions, longings, doubts, and frustrations as they come to mind. These questions may be helpful:
> — What is the call to service which is emerging for me —
>   with my partner or closest companion?
> — to my soul-friends?
> — to my Order or other covenant group?
> — to the Church?
> — to the needs of the World?

Remember that you are not called to do everything! Seek to discern your *charism* (gifts) and *apostolate* (what you are sent forth by God to do).

4. Prayer
In your prayer time, or as part of praying the Daily Office or celebrating the Eucharist, include the *Veni, Sancte Spiritus* found on page iii.

[Note: There is no meditation guide for Chapter Ten.]

Accountability   (Appendix B)

1. Prayer for Illumination
Pray that the Spirit will enable you to discover what God is calling you to be accountable about and who can help you with that accountability.

2. Listening for the Word of God
Read Ephesians 4:11-16.
What is God saying to you through this passage?

3. Reflection
At this point you may want to read and reflect on *The Rule of Life and Service* (Appendix A on page 112) or some other covenant of accountability.

Be open both to insights which witness to the Spirit at work within you, and to those which call you to account. Include your questions, longings, doubts, and frustrations as they come to mind. Let the Holy Spirit guide you to the accountability which God wants you to discover.

4. Prayer
In your prayer time, or as part of praying the Daily Office or celebrating the Eucharist, include the *Veni, Sancte Spiritus* found on page iii.